Egg on the Face

DEDICATION

*To those friends and colleagues
who have allowed their embarrassing moments
to be aired again in this book.*

Egg on the Face

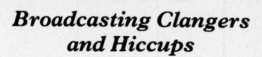

Broadcasting Clangers and Hiccups

Nicholas Parsons
and
Joy Leslie Gibson

Illustrations by Bill Tidy

Guild Publishing London

This edition published 1985 by
Book Club Associates
by arrangement with Weidenfeld & Nicolson

Published in Great Britain by
George Weidenfeld & Nicolson Limited

Printed in Great Britain by Butler & Tanner Ltd,
Frome and London

Contents

1 · Scrambled Egg

'Egg on the face' is an expression familiar to anyone in showbusiness and to no one more than myself. It seems that I have become so identified with on-the-air disaster, as listeners to *Just a Minute* will know, that I suppose it was natural the publishers should turn to me, an expert, to compile this book with Joy. My old friend John Morley, who has written more pantos than I have had hot dinners, tells me that whenever he is stuck for something to reduce the audience to hysterics he makes the ugly sisters or the demon king yell 'Nicholas Parsons!'. It ought to be all rather hurtful but over the years I have grown used to the fact that if custard pies had homing devices they would invariably find me.

'Egg on the face' is a clanger or technical hiccup that occurs in public and which makes the perpetrator months or even years later jerk out of dreamless sleep with sweat on the brow and heart pumping wildly. This book recalls some of those situations which we all experience at some time or other – remarks we make which seem so witty or apt at the time – but which, at least in our own eyes, make us feel very silly when we replay the scene in our minds. What makes it all so much worse for a broadcaster is that instead of making a fool of oneself before two or three people the 'egg on the face' has been applied to the delight of millions. Sometimes an actor or presenter will not be aware that something has gone wrong and continues blithely. It is only afterwards that he claps his hand to his forehead in horror when told what he has perpetrated. On other occasions he realises immediately

I

that something is amiss and tries desperately to retrieve the situation.

In recent years, with the advent of sophisticated recording equipment, nearly all entertainment programmes are pre-recorded and if anything goes wrong during the recording it can all be done over again or the mistake can be edited out later. Nowadays, therefore, most clangers or hiccups occur in actuality programmes, those shows which are transmitted 'live'. Let me add a note of confusion and say that many live shows are much less spontaneous and 'lively' than ... er ... dead – no, 'unlive' shows! The general public has become used so quickly to the technical wonders of the communications industry that people are surprised when you tell them that as recently as the 1960s nearly every programme on the television was 'live'. Almost all the shows that I did with that marvellous comedian, Arthur Haynes, were live – and doing a comedy show under those conditions is very challenging. Things frequently went wrong but we just covered as best we could and carried on. The audience loved it, and accepted it as part of the excitement of television – in fact, in our particular show they were disappointed if things did not go wrong. Nowadays, everything is so slick and the audience so aware, that if anything goes wrong it becomes an event.

I tried to discover how this expression, 'egg on the face', was coined – without much success. I think it could either have come from the white of egg that comedians used in the mixture they would throw at another artist's face in a slap-stick scene, since the phrase is nearly always prefaced with the words, 'He was left standing there with ....' Alternatively, it would come from the time when actors did sometimes have rotten eggs thrown at them. Fortunately that fate now seems to be reserved for those non-professional comedians: politicians.

As an actor and entertainer working a great deal in radio and television, I have experienced my fair share of 'egg'. One of the most embarrassing experiences I can remember was in the early 1950s when I worked with Eric Barker, a man with a brilliantly inventive comic mind, who wrote and starred in his own television series. He was responsible for the first satirical sketches on television – though it was not called satire in those days. All the satirical comedy – or 'send up' – shows that have followed are really only developments or variations of what he pioneered on television. I was privileged at a very young age to be working with such a talented man. The sketches, which were usually take-offs of current television shows, were interspersed with a song or a dance routine. This not only made a good variety programme, but gave the actors a chance to change their clothes between sketches. The show was live, of course, and the cameras were not as mobile or sophisticated as today. It was all transmitted from the main studio at Lime Grove, which was the home of all BBC television then, and the final rehearsal was undertaken as much to see if the cameras could move from one set in the studio to another, as to discover if the artists could make the necessary changes, and the stage staff silently dismantle one set and replace it with another in the allotted time. The changes of clothes for different sketches were made behind the 'flats', the scenery in front of which the actors performed. Eric was rather short-sighted and after one sketch in which he didn't wear his specs, he was looking for his dresser to help him make a quick change. He failed to notice that the cameras were filming on a certain set, and instead of walking behind the flats, walked in front dressed in outrageous football gear while Janet Brown was singing a song about doing the housework. The viewers must have been very puzzled but there is no time to explain in a live show, you just carry on.

The embarrassing situation I experienced was during a quick change I was making behind one of the flats of a set from where the action was then being transmitted. A camera, being pushed rapidly by the cameraman from one set to the next, knocked this flat over. I was revealed in the middle of an elegant dance routine, in my underwear, with another man – the dresser – taking off my clothes in what must have looked a very compromising way. It destroyed

3

the dance routine and did little for my personal reputation, as the show had to keep going and no explanation could be given for my seemingly strange behaviour and unconventional tastes.

That was just the beginning. In a varied career in the world of broadcasting I have wondered if I were not the kind of character who had almost permanent egg on his face. For ten years with Arthur Haynes, as his straight man, I was the butt for his humour, and in the sketches we performed I was regularly made to look foolish. In *Just a Minute* on radio, which has been running now for seventeen years, I am 'put-down' by the regular panelists with complete disregard for my feelings as a 'sensitive plant among the cacti'. After *Sale of the Century* became a success, the press joined in. It is odd how the critics resent popular programmes. Then, when I appeared in the Tyne Tees variety series for Channel 4, *Super Troupers*, I was cast in the role of 'the chaser', who is booed off the stage at the end of each show. You could say I have earned a living by having egg literally spread on my face. Next time you ladle scrambled eggs on to hot buttered toast you might like to remember that for most of the time I feel like the toast.

How do you like your egg cooked?

There are different kinds of 'eggs'. There are the verbal ones – when the person realises afterwards he has dropped a clanger, and doesn't know which way to look. It is even worse when the clanger is spoken to camera – as when Frank Bough, after Fanny Cradock had finished one of her cooking shows, said to the viewers, 'Let's hope all *your* doughnuts come out as Fanny's.'

Another 'egg' situation is the one I call the 'human hiccup', and can easily arise in broadcasting when the programme is live. It is nothing to do with the person in front of the camera but it is his face that gets covered in egg. Peter Woods was fronting the nine o'clock news on the BBC one night when he picked up a piece of paper which had been hastily handed to him with the latest football results on it. He looked at the piece of paper, paused, then looked up and said to the viewers, 'I'm sorry, I can't read it. The handwriting is so bad.'

In contrast to this there is the 'egg' situation in a live show when the audience is not aware of a problem but the performer is and can see disaster creeping nearer without being able to do anything about it. Actress Wendy Padbury had a tussle with a real egg. She was performing in a television play in the days when everything went out live, and had to eat a boiled egg. During rehearsals she had just mimed this with an empty shell. On transmission a real boiled egg was put in front of her on the table, and on cue she cracked it open, only to find to her horror that the egg was bad. She carried on with the performance, eating some of the egg as best she could, and giving every appearance that she was enjoying it. At the end of the scene she had to dash to the ladies' loo.

The 'egg' which occurs as a result of a technical hiccup over which the actor has no control is less likely to occur today when, as I have explained, most programmes are pre-recorded and meticulously timed. When Independent Television began there were many serious programmes planned, and 'classic drama' was allotted a large share of peak-time. One prestigious undertaking was an all-star production of Shakespeare's *Hamlet*. It was a solemn and almost sacred occasion – commerce's proud offering to the god of culture. All went well and it proceeded majestically to its inevitable tragic climax. Then as Fortinbras stepped forward to speak the final lines of the play, the screen dissolved, and a jingle cut across the dignified appeal for four soldiers to carry Hamlet to his tomb and a row of dancing oranges appeared advertising a well-known drink.

There is an 'egg' situation which is entirely technical, and neither the audience nor the technicians are aware of it. On Radio 3 there was a programme devoted to modern music, and a tape of a composition by Margaret Sambell was played backwards. There were no complaints from the listeners, and it seems only the composer herself was aware of the hiccup which had occurred.

There is also another kind of 'egg' that only occurred in the early days of broadcasting, when the 'wireless' was an innocent and unsophisticated pastime requiring little in the way of expertise from its practitioners except self-confidence. In some ways everything was much more lackadaisical in those days. There was far less money available for one thing, but there were very strict rules to which everyone rigidly adhered, about what could or could not be said on air. In particular, it was absolutely forbidden to mention brand names. Anything that smacked of advertising was an anathema. A good example of this was when the racing correspondent, R. C. Lyle, was giving a commentary on the Derby. At one point he said, 'The horses are now passing the advertisement hoarding for Booth's Dry Gin.' Sir John Reith, the dignified and austere Director-General of the BBC, was horrified; not only by the commentary, but also because Gordon's Gin rang up to protest and ask for a similar comment for themselves.

The clangers and hiccups that occur in radio today often result from the pressure of long stints on duty in a live show. This can give rise to the kind of 'egg' where the broadcaster is almost aware that he is making a mistake as he is speaking but is too late to check himself. This is what happened to Don Durbridge who now works for Invicta Radio in Kent. Before that he was a newsreader on Radio 2 and often had the early morning duty from five o'clock to eight. This is a difficult time of the day in which to be alert and wide awake. On this occasion, Don had come to the end of the last news bulletin he was to read that day, the eight o'clock. As he says himself: 'Once you reach eight o'clock you feel you have cracked it. It's the last bulletin you will be reading that day, and most of the items are the same as in previous bulletins. Perhaps you relax a little, the concentration is not so intense, and that is when those embarrassing moments occur.' It was the last item in the news bulletin, and it was about Spain which that day had become a democracy after forty years under Franco. 'Finally (Don told the nation), today, thirty-eight million Spaniards have been experiencing their first erection for forty years.' Terry Wogan came straight over the top of this statement with his usual wit to comment: 'British Airways announce that all flights to Spain are now fully booked!'

Phone-in programmes are, of course, a wonderful source for blush-making moments. On a morning radio show the presenter asked a listener who had phoned in to name a record she would like, and added, 'What would you enjoy most?' '*Feeling* by Des O'Connor,' she replied without hesitation.

There have been a number of broadcasting firsts, especially in the early days, when someone finished up with 'egg on the face', and most of them are in this book. There was, however, one broadcasting first which was unique since on this occasion everyone in the studio had 'egg on their faces', except the person responsible for creating the situation. Kenneth Tynan, the distinguished critic and professional *enfant terrible* had deliberately come on television to shock, and make his own personal contribution, as he saw it, to breaking down prudery and hypocrisy. Bernard Shaw had the same idea when he put the word 'bloody' into Eliza's mouth in *Pygmalion*. This was the first time 'bloody' had been spoken on stage and a delightful *frisson* went through the audience who were able to feel shocked and daring at the same time. I remember as a youngster seeing the film of *Pygmalion* in the 1940s starring Wendy Hillier, and when she said 'bloody', even then it had an electric effect on the cinema audience. On television, Tynan achieved the same effect by casually saying a word absolutely forbidden to broadcasters. The moment occurred in *TW3* – that splendid and much missed satirical programme *That Was The Week That Was*. Tynan was being interviewed by Robert Robinson, and they were discussing censorship. Tynan without any embarrassment and quite deliberately, used a certain four-letter word for the first time in public. He said that he didn't think that it would be

long before 'fuck' would be used quite naturally in plays where the playwright thought it necessary. There was dead silence in the studio. In the control room you could have heard a pin drop. At the end of the discussion, Ned Sherrin, who was in charge of the programme, said, 'I suppose that's some kind of first.' The papers gave it headlines and enjoyed being shocked. Many viewers were horrified, indignant, or just plain embarrassed. Tynan certainly achieved what he set out to do and what he prophesied has slowly come about. Today, however, I sometimes wonder if too many four-letter words aren't somewhat tedious to listen to, and unnecessary when an alternative phrase can often have more impact. If everything becomes acceptable, it will be rather sad, and we will miss a lot of fun, and those embarrassing moments when verbal clangers are dropped would no longer be amusing.

Human nature being what it is, we seem to laugh loudest at other people's misfortune. We find it funny when someone else has 'egg on the face' particularly on television or radio where everyone seems so fluent, so in control. Is it possible, one sometimes asks oneself, that Robert Robinson will one day dry up or Richard Baker lose his cool? Here we recall some of those delightful moments when things did not go quite as planned, and suddenly those skilled professionals we watch on our television and listen to on our radio, hardly hesitating, repeating themselves or deviating from the script or the subject on their cue-cards, just for a minute had 'egg on their face'.

2 · In the Beginning

In the early days of broadcasting, clangers and hiccups were more likely to happen than now. There was not the sophisticated machinery with which people can be quickly cut-off, faded out, or otherwise stopped from broadcasting anything disastrous. By today's standards, some unbelievable broadcasting disasters were not only aired but allowed to linger in the ether long after they ought to have been 'faded'. One of the most famous, certainly one of the longest, of these involved a commentator called Commander Tommy Woodroffe. The occasion was the Royal Naval Review at Spithead in 1935. Commander Woodroffe had been sent by the BBC to Spithead to cover the event for the 'wireless'. The highlight of the review was to be the illumination of the fleet as darkness fell and which Woodroffe was to describe. He spent the day on board his old ship, H.M.S. *Nelson*, enjoying some of that hospitality for which the Royal Navy is famous. Eventually the time came for Tommy Woodroffe to broadcast, and commentate 'live' as the various warships switched on their lights. Unfortunately by this time Tommy's speech was not only blurred, his sight was none too clear either. It seems the only person unaware of this was Tommy himself.

'The fleet's lit up (he began bravely but ambiguously). When I say lit up, I mean lit up by fairy lights ... it isn't a fleet at all ... the whole fleet is fairyland. If you follow me through ... if you don't mind ... when I say "the fleet's lit up" I mean the whole ships ... (very long pause).... I was telling someone to shut up. The whole fleet's lit up ... the ship's lit up ... even the destroyers are lit up....

We are going to fire a rocket ... we are going to fire all
sorts of things ... you may hear my reaction when I see
them.... A huge fleet here ... a colossal fleet lit up with
fairy lights.... The whole thing is fairyland ... it isn't true
... it's gone, it's gone ... it's disappeared (mournfully)....
No magician ever waved his wand with more acumen. The
fleet's gone ... it's disappeared.... I'm trying to give you
ladies and gentlemen a description.... The fleet's gone ...
it's disappeared ... the whole thing's gone.... They've disappeared ... we have two hundred warships all round
us.... Now they've all gone.... There's nothing between
us and heaven ... there's nothing at all.'

Eventually someone in charge became aware of what was
happening and the broadcast was faded and they 'returned
to the studio'. After the broadcast, Lord Reith, who was not
exactly famous for his sense of humour, rather his lack of
it, laid into poor Tommy for all he was worth. The unfortunate Commander was suspended for six months and was
lucky not to be sacked. He was also on occasions reprimanded for not giving enough details on his expenses
sheets, one of which read: 'refreshments to the Clerk of the
Course, the Judge, the Starter, and the gentleman with
glasses wearing a pin-striped suit whose name I didn't quite
catch'.

For Lord Reith the BBC was not a suitable venue for
stand-up comedy, particularly when something sacred such
as royalty or the navy was involved. It is a little sad to think
that today Tommy would have been cut-off after a
few seconds and not allowed to delight listeners for several
minutes.

One of the early broadcasters was A. J. Alan, who used
to tell stories. He was not only successful at this, he was
also successful in an entirely different way. He was one of
the few people who managed to take alcohol into a studio.
In those days, the 1920s, it was strictly taboo. Alcohol was
never supposed to be on the premises. Nevertheless, A.J.
would arrive with a small attache case, out of which he
would take a flask of brandy, which he placed on one side

of the microphone; his script came out next, each sheet of paper gummed on to cardboard, so there would be no rustle of paper as he spoke – a true broadcasting professional. Next would come a pencil, an india rubber, and a stop-watch. Since someone had once told him that the ideal distance from which to speak into a microphone was eighteen inches, a steel tape-measure was then produced, and Alan would measure the distance exactly. Finally, he would take out a candle and a box of matches, and solemnly light the candle. Apparently, once, in an earlier broadcast, the lights had failed while Alan was on the air, so now he made sure that he could go on reading whatever happened! For Alan, alcohol was the oil he needed to make his stories flow but he never fell into Tommy Woodroffe's condition. He was far too professional.

In the early days of broadcasting, commentaries were not always done directly from the ground where the sport was taking place. The BBC had not yet risen to the sophistication of having commentary boxes, and all the expense which went with such complicated paraphernalia. The commentator would arrive at the ground, go to a nearby house, which had been hastily borrowed by the BBC, and the summary of the match would be broadcast from a convenient vantage point in that house or on its roof, with the commentator having to cope as well as he could following the game through binoculars. Howard Marshall, one of the earliest cricket commentators, and extremely good at his job, was dismayed to find that when he had located the house from which he was to broadcast a cricket match, his commentary was going to have to compete with the young daughter of that house having her piano lesson. His engineer asked the child if she would stop, to which she readily agreed. I imagine anything to get out of her piano lesson. Howard Marshall continued with his broadcast when suddenly the door of the room was flung open, and he was accosted by the girl's mother who shouted loud enough for all the listeners to hear, 'How much longer are you going on? My little girl's wasting her music lesson!'

Another classic clanger from the early days of broadcasting reflects the less sophisticated world that existed before the War. Weary as we are today of advertising with sexual undertones, simulated sex on stage, and comic sketches based on the *double entendre*, it is hard to capture the innocence of audience and broadcasters alike fifty years ago. The broadcast concerned Isobel Anne Shead who was telling a story on the much-loved children's programme *Listen with Mother*.

The announcer at the time was Michael Brooke. His name was actually Reginald Brooke, but the BBC thought that Reginald was a little bit pompous for an announcer so he changed it to Reggie Brooke. He was then told that 'Reggie' was far too low-brow so he took his son's name of Michael. In those days announcers had responsibility for checking scripts and censoring them if necessary. When Michael Brooke read the script that Isobel Anne Shead had prepared for *Listen with Mother*, he was worried about how it would be received. He took it to Tom Chalmers, who was then Head of Sound and pointed out that it could be taken to be salacious. On the other hand, there was nothing obviously censorable in the dialogue and the *double entendres* were quite unintentional. Neither man wished to try and explain to Miss Shead that the whole of her script was full of double meanings and could be completely misunderstood. It was decided eventually to leave it, on the basis that as it had been written in innocence it should be received in that way. This script discussion within the department meant that the engineers had heard that something unusual was embodied in what should have been a very innocent story for very young children. So alerted, the actual programme was recorded by them for posterity.

Miss Shead on the programme invited the children to imagine that they were at a party: 'I want you to imagine you have all got balls. When the music is low your balls are on the ground and when the music is high, jump up and throw your balls in the air. Now let's play with each other's balls – isn't that fun. . . .' She continued in this vein for a full five minutes and caused considerable mirth among the technicians, and presumably some adults listening. I believe, however, Miss Shead was never herself made aware of what amusement her broadcast had caused.

Censorship on radio in the early days was very strict but sometimes unpredictable. Much of it was left rather oddly to the programme announcers who had the responsibility for removing anything which was deemed unsuitable. This meant that some things were passed that might be considered *risqué* while on occasions quite innocent things were taken out. There is one story of an announcer who obviously knew very little about the history of fashion. In one script he came across the expression 'period dress', and in his innocence thought that this referred to the clothes that women wore at a certain period of the month, and immediately cut it out of the script.

BBC radio remained very censorious about what could be said on the radio right into the late 1950s. It was felt that unlike going to the theatre – a deliberate choice – the radio came into everyone's home almost regardless of whether people liked it or not and had therefore a responsibility not to shock even the youngest listener. When I was broadcasting a lot in the 1950s, all producers were circulated with a list of words, in strict alphabetical order, which on no account were to be used. It made strange reading since it contained every rude word the BBC had ever heard of, a litany in alphabetical order that began with 'arse' and ended with 'yoni'. Among the truly offensive expressions were included positively lady-like exclamations such as darn, damn and damnation. Even ruddy was frowned upon so actors had to get a lot of expression into words like dash, or phrases like 'darn it'.

There was an occasion when I was telling a joke in a variety programme, and the pay-off was that the girl in the story was standing naked in a casino. Naked was another taboo word – it was suggestive of sex which was forbidden. By now – in the 1950s – the producer had overall responsibility for making decisions about which words were included in a script – though he could refer to a higher authority when in doubt. He suggested that I say 'the girl had nothing on'. This sounded so flat, that it killed the joke. It had to be one word, so a compromise was reached, and I was allowed to say 'starkers'. It meant the same, sounded acceptable and was not on the list of censored words, and fortunately it also raised a laugh!

Oliver Wakefield was a popular comedian in the 1930s. He had a very individual style and a very English accent. He employed hesitation in his delivery for effect, non-sequitors in his stories, and a tendency to stutter and stumble over words. It could be very funny and I remember one broadcast he did in *Music Hall*, the famous variety show which followed *In Town Tonight* every Saturday evening. He stuttered over a word beginning with the letter 'p' so it sounded as though he had said 'pee'. It seems unbelievable now but this made headlines in the popular press and the BBC actually banned him from broadcasting.

Not only was there a list of forbidden words, but there were five subjects which were absolutely taboo and could not be referred to on the air. The subjects were: profanity or mention of the deity; the Royal Family; physical disability; racial remarks; and sexual deviation. This inspired a wonderful sentence, attributed to those witty writers Frank Muir and Denis Norden, which covered all the taboo subjects mentioned – and in the order listed. The sentence ran as follows: ' "Jesus Christ," said the Queen, "I do believe that one-legged darky is a poof!" '

Ian Messiter, that brilliant inventor of radio panel games and quiz shows – including *Just a Minute*, worked on the permanent staff of the BBC in the early days. One of his first jobs was to put on the records in music shows. The expression 'disc jockey' had not yet been invented and the programme presenters were almost always staff announcers chosen for their voices rather than their wit. It seems strange now but the announcers pre-recorded introductions to the records which would then be inserted before the record was played. Ian was called an RPA (Recorded Programme Assistant), his pay was £2·50 a week, and the announcers, who seemed to him veritable giants of broadcasting, were not paid much more. To set up a programme, it was necessary to go with a list of the music you wanted to the Recorded Programmes Library, draw out the records and then go to another section of the library and draw out the numbered recorded introductions to match the discs. Next the RPA had to find a little playback room and listen to the discs and the announcements to make sure they matched. When the programme was for what is now the BBC's World Service the RPA would have to choose the correct foreign language version of the introduction to put with the record he had selected. This meant listening carefully for a title that sounded something like the one written on the disc. For instance, although Ian knew only ten words of Italian, it was relatively simple to identify the title of the record in the Italian announcer's introduction to it. Hindustani proved to be more difficult.

One evening it happened. Ian found himself with a whole package of Indian discs for a two-hour programme. The linking material had been recorded in Hindustani of which Ian was quite ignorant. He had half an hour to check the two-hour programme, so he went to the Indian section but unluckily there was no one there at that particular moment with any knowledge of the language. Ian had never made a mistake before. The disc numbers had always tallied with the announcement numbers so rather than hang about waiting for the right person to turn up he went to the studio hoping the engineer in charge would be Hindustani. He was not. He was a Scot. He took a chance.

Days went by. These turned to weeks. Nothing happened. At the beginning of the fourth week when the whole incident was forgotten, the head of the service was seen to come down to the RPA's room and check in the logbook. Ian Messiter was there at the time sitting on an old sofa on which the RPAs sometimes slept when working nights.

The Very Important Indian looked up from the log-book and asked, 'Do any of you know Messiter?'

'I'm Messiter, sir.'

'Come to my office, if you please.'

He went. The Indian waved his hand at an armchair filled with letters which had been dumped there. They spread over the floor too. There must have been several hundreds of them. They meant nothing to Messiter, so he asked what they were about. Apparently he had been playing announcements which introduced discs listeners had heard the previous week. For this fiasco Ian was transferred to another section of the BBC where almost unbelievably, he was given the same job but this time the language he had to wrestle with was Dutch of which again he knew not a word.

Naturally Ian kept an eye on the notice board offering jobs to BBC employees within the organisation. Eventually he applied for the job of Variety Producer. (These people are now called Light Entertainment Producers.) He went before an awesome board but got the job – no extra money until he had held the post for a year; as it turned out he stayed longer.

There was a very fine pianist called Ivor Dennis and as Ian Messiter could not read music he was told to produce a show featuring Dennis. This is not such a silly idea as it at first seems, at least from Ivor Dennis's point of view, because it meant Ian, the Producer, could not interfere. Furthermore, the linking announcements between the music was done by the announcer so really Ian had little to do. They were up at Broadcasting House in a studio. The fifteen-minute programme was a weekly affair with no audience so they used a little studio which just about fitted the Steinway 'grand', the piano microphone, and the Announcer's microphone. Ian was in charge, which meant little except that he had to time the programme and make sure it ran fourteen minutes and thirty seconds. Ivor had rehearsed and chosen his music several days before. He didn't, however, have a stopwatch. Ian had a BBC watch, so in his own words, 'I could play at being a producer'. There was little he could contribute. He had not chosen Ivor; he had not chosen the music; but he had a stopwatch which he wore on an impressive black ribbon round his neck for much the same reason that a young inexperienced doctor wears his stethoscope.

'We were engaged in running the music through and timing it to fit,' Ian recalls. 'The programme was not to be recorded. It was to go out live. Rehearsal over. The red light went on. We were on the air. The announcer announced. Ivor played and we were about six minutes into the programme when in came a studio attendant in a brown coat carrying a vacuum cleaner which he plugged in and switched on.

'I have never moved so fast. I left the control room and was in the studio unplugging the cleaner within three seconds, at the same time signalling to the attendant not to speak and pointing to the red light. He seemed unaware of the microphones and was standing by the announcer's mike as he produced a piece of paper.

' "Look!" he said, pointing a stubby, grubby finger at his paper. "I'm in the right studio." According to the paper, he was. "I got my instructions." He was obviously not going to get out of the studio and we were still on the air. He was bending down to replug the vacuum cleaner. I told him I was sorry, but there must be a mistake as we were broadcasting live.

' "Oh, very well, I'll get on with the next studio." He picked up his machine. As he went towards the door he turned round looking at me, but speaking directly into the announcer's mike again, to give me his parting shot.

' "Too much bloody broadcasting going on here." '

'Oh yes, we had letters. Lots of them.'

In those days the 'wireless' was everything. The number of TV sets was so small they did not count. TV air time was occupied more often than not by the card reading: NORMAL SERVICE WILL BE RESUMED AS SOON AS POSSIBLE than by the programmes that were supposed to occupy

the one station for two hours each evening. The best entertainment was on radio and on radio the greatest entertainment was *ITMA*, *It's That Man Again* starring Tommy Handley and produced by Francis Worsley. It started in 1939 and finished in 1949 with the death of the star.

It is difficult to imagine at this distance what its influence was. It was full of catch phrases and every family 'funny' man would use them at the slightest excuse. 'I don't mind if I do.' 'Can I do you now, Sir?' 'It's being so cheerful as keeps me going.' 'I'm going down now, Sir.' 'Fumph speaking', etc. No radio or TV series before or since has ever had such an audience or impact. Before we leave Ian Messiter he must just be allowed to recall his very special memory of that programme.

'Because my father was a doctor and he would often try to talk to patients who had the "wireless" permanently on, he refused to have one in the house. When Mother insisted on having a wireless at the outbreak of war, my father would hear the six o'clock time pips, look at his watch and say that the BBC should get a better clock as they were always two or three minutes out. It was the same with the newsreaders. "Yes," he would say, "but the BBC employs actors to do all that. Actors cannot be trusted. Wait until we see it in print tomorrow in *The Times*. His dislike of the wireless meant that I had never heard *ITMA*, and in 1948 shortly after I was married, the Head of Variety asked me to go to his office.

'Francis Worsley had been taken ill. I had produced a few shows without disaster. Would I produce *ITMA* until Francis came back? It wasn't so much "Would you?" but "You will". I ran back to my office and telephoned my wife at home. "What's ITMA?" I asked. She told me it was probably the greatest show ever. I was terrified. I had never heard of Tommy Handley. The build-up he was given by my wife, who spoke his name in hushed tones of reverence, frightened me. I asked one or two other producers about the show and carefully concealed my ignorance. They, too, were almost on their knees at the mention of the show. I was really frightened. Then came the first meeting with Tommy Handley who could see I was young, the youngest Variety Producer ever, and he put me at my ease at once. "Don't worry. Just time the run-through. Allow four minutes for laughter and applause. Give me a signal at three minutes to the end. I will wind up in time for the closing announcements and signature tune."

'I did just that. I have no idea what the show was about. I was too scared to listen.

'John Watt, Head of Variety, stopped me the next day as I passed his office door, "Well done!" he said.

'But I still don't know what it was I'd done, but it was a good thing I had remembered to wind up my stopwatch.'

Vera Lynn, now Dame Vera, was extremely popular during the War, being given the soubriquet of the Forces' Sweetheart – but her popularity was hard won, not everyone liking her style of singing. The then Deputy Director of the BBC, Sir Cecil Graves, once asked, 'Why should we hear so much of Vera Lynn? How could men fit themselves for battles with these debilitating tunes in their ears? The BBC cannot avoid some responsibility for making this lady popular and so for lowering the morale of fighting men. Besides, the theme of most of these songs is sentimental sex and this mood at the best of times should not be encouraged.' This was at the time when Vera's popularity was immense. Letters would arrive from every type of serviceman who would request songs to be sung to their loved ones. Howard Thomas, the Producer, had the courage to continue employing Vera Lynn, and if anyone was left with egg on the face it was Sir Cecil Graves.

Phyllis Dixey who was a very successful striptease dancer, was in real life a very 'proper' person. During the War she was very popular with the troops. Stripping regularly, and by today's standards very tastefully, at the Whitehall Theatre. Howard Thomas decided that he should include her in a programme for the Merchant Navy called *Shipmates Ashore* which was broadcast live. Phyllis couldn't do

a striptease on the air, so she sang a song, one verse of which went something like this:

> I'm not lovely like Frances Day
> Who can dance and sing and play,
> I have the boys in my dressing-room
> And give them tea and crumpet.

This brought a telephone call to Thomas from the Controller of the BBC.

'Crumpet? You know what that means?'

'Of course,' said Thomas innocently, 'something you have for tea. It was passed by the Censor.' The Controller replied ominously, 'You will hear more of this.' Eventually Thomas received a reprimand which contained this gem, 'If crumpet had been used in the plural there would have been no objection!'

Howard Thomas later moved to television and was working for ABC TV in an executive capacity, when one Sunday night, while watching a production of an *Armchair Theatre* play, the Manager in charge of the studio contacted him by telephone, while the play was in progress, and in an anxious whisper, stated: 'One of the actors has just died and is lying on the studio floor. What shall I do?' Thomas replied: 'Get him out of the picture and get on with the play.' Which is what happened, the other actors carrying on as best they could leaving the audience rather confused about the end of the play!

Many years ago, when Michael Aspel was a newsreader, he was playing cricket for charity when a ball hit his toecap and ricocheted straight into his eye. It became very swollen and bruised and the next day, when he went to the TV studios to read the news, he asked the make-up girl if she could do anything to disguise it, and was disconcerted to hear her say: 'I prefer it to the other one – the colours are quite sexy!' The eye made international news – even the American magazine *Time* commented: 'Last night on BBC TV, Michael Aspel read the news with his usual impeccable accent. His tie was straight, he showed just the right amount of cuff; in fact he was just what the British expect of their newsreaders – apart from one feature: he had a black eye. Even the manner in which he got it was typically British. "A cricket ball hit me," he said.'

Robert Dougall, who read the news on television with such style over many years, started with the old BBC Empire Service and was often on night duty. He sometimes finished broadcasting at 1.30 a.m. in the morning, and then had to be on again at 6 a.m. the same day. Announcers doing this stint would be given a bed in an office and would be called by telephone. It wasn't an ideal place to have a few hours' sleep, and sometimes the Duty Announcer would just drop off only minutes, it seemed, before the telephone shrilled in his ear. This happened often to Bob, and one day, having answered the telephone, he went straight off to sleep again and wasn't finally roused until an irate engineer, who had just opened the lines into the studio where Bob was meant to be, realised he wasn't there to make the opening announcement. Hurriedly a record was put on, Bob re-awakened, and still in pyjamas and dressing-gown he raced into the studio.

When writing up the log-book as he came off duty, Bob idly turned back to the preceding day to find that his colleague Basil Gray had done the same thing, and previously the third announcer Joe Shewen had also had the same experience!

Lionel Marson was the announcer on duty when the Stone of Scone was stolen from Westminster Abbey. He was reading the news calmly, just finishing up when another item was thrust at him. Not being able to read it over, Lionel began reading the message quite fluently, ending with, 'The stone has rested in the Abbey since the days of Edward Isst.' He felt somewhat puzzled not remembering who Edward Isst was! Then the duty editor pointed frantically at the word, and Lionel said, 'I am sorry, I should have said Edward Iced!'

The radio programme *Down Your Way*, which is now compèred by Brian Johnston, was originally handled by

Stewart MacPherson. In the early days of radio he used to knock on doors and conduct interviews on the spot. Nowadays the programme is carefully researched, and the interviewees selected. In those early days it was very haphazard and entirely spontaneous. The programme visits a different town each week, and on one occasion Stewart MacPherson knocked on a door and when it was opened said, 'Is Mrs Brown in?' The man who had answered the door said, 'Oh, you are the chap who has been after my missus' and punched him in the face.

3 · *Spoonerisms, Bawdy Bits and Hoaxes*

Broadcasting is the perfect place to perpetrate spoonerisms. The Rev Dr Spooner is supposed to have invented or given his name to this verbal slip where words become transposed, and allows broadcasters to talk about Ugasian Andans, shattered scowers of rain, dam bomage and the star-bangled spanner. Older radio listeners will perhaps remember 'the interlush by Ernest Lude', and being told, 'We are now going to hear a programme of light music from the Bathroom in Pump.'

A memorable spoonerism many years ago went: 'Our next programme features Mr Peabody on the pianoforte. Yes, Mr Playbody is going to pee for you.'

In one famous radio production of *Macbeth*, the listeners were amazed to hear Lady Macbeth say 'stick your courage to the screwing place'. Having now heard that, I am not sure I would ever be confident of saying that line right. I expect, however, it will be some time before I am asked to play that role.

In the late 1940s I actually heard an announcer introduce that wonderful pianist Charlie Kuntz – pronounced Koons – as one might expect it to be pronounced. More recently, during the hunt for the horrific rapist known as the Black Panther, a Radio 2 newsreader announced: 'Following a tip-off, the police are hopeful that they may be closer to discovering the whereabouts of the Pink Panther.'

In January 1985 on *The World at One* Brian Widlake,

talking about victory in Europe, referred to VD day – and no doubt there was some of that about too.

One of the most delightful spoonerisms was the work of an American presenter, who, after a recorded symphony concert, concluded with the words, 'The conductor was Otosco Tiscanini. I mean Atisco Tiscanoni, I mean Arturo Toscanini.' There was a long pause, then he said, 'My name is Ben Graver, ladies and gentlemen. Remember it well, because you'll probably never hear it again. . . .' Hundreds of viewers rang urging that Graver should not be fired. He wasn't. All of which goes to prove that the general public enjoy mistakes. If you have established yourself as a smooth and efficient presenter, then the occasional clanger only endears you to the viewing or listening public.

The charming and normally ice-cool Angela Rippon was reading the news once and referred to the government's pay guidelines as 'the government's gay pielines'.

In the USA during the Pope's visit a newsreader referred to him as 'His Poopiness the Hole'.

Christopher Martin-Jenkins, sports commentator, seeing a bald man in the crowd described him as our bald-freddied hen and though sport is excellent for finding commentators speaking too fast for their tongues it is newsreading that provides the most pleasure. How could one not be delighted by the newsreader who assured us that President Reagan was 'alive and kicking two-and-a-half months into his pregnancy'.

I was responsible for a clanger some years ago, much cherished by the team on *Just a Minute*. The four regular panelists, when they have exhausted their wit and inventiveness on the subject they are discussing, invariably find it a good ploy to turn on their chairman. On this particular occasion the subject was 'snapshots', and Kenneth Williams was giving me a particularly difficult time. Then Derek Nimmo and Peter Jones joined in the fun of harassing me. In my efforts to call them to order and continue with the game, I insisted that I would not allow the challenge, disagreed with the arguments, and would they please restrain

themselves, adding that 'Clement Freud now had the subject and it was snopshats ... snipshots ... snopshits ... snip ... snop ... snap ...' I was reassured after the programme was transmitted, to receive a letter from a Professor of English at Aberdeen University who said he felt that I had enriched the language.

Sex is the bane of the broadcaster's life. Not sex itself but 'talking dirty' quite inadvertently. I heard one of these clangers quite recently on Radio 4. The announcer who was linking programmes during the morning said, 'Do you know what a frigger is? If you don't, tune in this afternoon to *Talking About Antiques*, and Arthur Negus will tell you.'

Another clanger which comes under this heading was perpetrated by television's weatherman, Tony Target, who, on the *Points West* programme, after calling a colleague by the wrong name, exclaimed, 'Oh, bugger!' This was thought worthy of being reported in the national press. Fortunately for Tony Target, in these more enlightened days, the television company defended him on the grounds that we all make mistakes. In the early days of broadcasting he might well have been sacked. One could almost see the egg on poor Tony's face when he realised what he had said.

Another unintentional bit of bawdiness was recalled for me by John Benson, the man who supplies the voice on *Sale of the Century*. He was working as a Station Announcer at the time, and a young Julian Pettifer had just joined the Company to do a similar job. A caption had appeared on the screen across the weather forecast, which was supposed to read 'Fog in the South, Rain later'. Unfortunately, the letter 'F' was missing from the word 'Fog', and when the Station Announcer, in the form of Pettifer, came on screen, he said, 'Well, that was the forecast and we're sorry for the F in Fog.' (You have to say that aloud!)

Lord Reith, the dignified and puritanical Director-General of the BBC in its early days, did have a sense of humour despite rumours to the contrary. He once received a letter from a lady who said she was horrified when switching on her radio to hear someone saying, 'Great tits like coconuts.' The outraged lady turned her set off and wrote her letter. Sir John made an investigation and wrote back, 'Dear Madam, If you had only continued listening you would have heard that robins like worms!'

In 1974 during the three-day week, Edward Heath, then Prime Minister, commanded that all three television channels should close down at 10.30 p.m. but the Water Board asked that this should be rescinded in favour of staggered closing. There was such a call for water at 10.30 in the evening with people going to the lavatories, having baths, using kettles of water for bed-time drinks and bottles, that the water system couldn't cope!

Going back to sport, where there is ample opportunity for misunderstanding and unfortunate remarks, an ABC Commentator was heard exclaiming during a cycling race in the Olympic Games, 'The one who's out in front is breaking a lot of wind.' Brian Johnston, many people's favourite cricket commentator, has in his time made quite a few unintentionally bawdy remarks. Here are some to which he admits: At the Headingley Test, 1961, 'There's Neil Harvey, standing at slip with his legs wide apart, waiting for a tickle.' 'Henry Horton's got a funny sort of stance. It looks as if he is shitting on a sooting stick.' 'As you come over to join us, Ray Illingworth has just relieved himself at the Pavilion end.' '. . . you've just missed seeing Barry Richards hit one of Basil D'Oliveira's balls clean out of the ground.' 'The bowler's Holding the batsman's Willey.'

Don Mosey was startled once to find the following cue card stuck in front of him: WELCOME LISTENERS IN THE VIRGIN ISLANDS, AND EXPLAIN THAT THEIR POSITION IS SOME CONSIDERABLE DISTANCE FROM THE ISLE OF MAN. Rex Alston, another well-known cricket commentator, during the tea interval at a match in Canterbury, is responsible for this unfortunate bit of phraseology: '. . . the band playing, people picnicking round the ground while on the field hundreds of small boys are playing with their balls.'

John Oaksey was giving the commentary at a York race meeting where the Clerk of the Course, a Major Petch, had

had built a concrete bank round the paddock so that more people could see the horses. John cued his cameras in with these immortal words: 'So let's look at Major Petch's erection – or perhaps I should call it Major Petch's stand!'

An unintentionally bawdy remark on television usually seems worse than when a radio commentator makes a mistake because one can actually see the expression on the face of the broadcaster. Jimmy Hill, that all-round sportsman who is so admirably authoritative when telling us what has happened on *Match of the Day*, once described the rugby football player Nigel Starmers-Smith as 'having had seven craps for England'.

Jimmy takes a certain pride in one of his best verbal slips. At least he honestly owns up to this marvellous clanger. It was the end of his programme, and indeed the end of the evening's viewing. It was Saturday and British Summer Time was due to end on Sunday. Jimmy rounding off his commentary, said 'Good-night', and then added this immortal piece of advice: 'And, don't forget tonight to put your cocks back.'

Royal Tours, like all events surrounded by pomp and ceremony, make perfect showcases for 'remarks-I-wish-I-had-never-said'. Godfrey Talbot in India with the Queen had to commentate from an insecure perch on an elephant. Insecure as he was, he can be forgiven for saying: 'Her Majesty, Head of the Commonwealth, sits entwined with the Maharajah.'

They do things even better in Africa where in Sierra Leone the radio commentator exclaimed: 'Oh my goodness, this is a wonderful thing we are seeing. Mrs Queen is so decent.'

Prince Philip was once described by a commentator as being in his sailor suit. While on another occasion, in Guyana, the woman commentator said that he was 'a dish' and finished thus: 'When the Royal pair left the garden at midnight, after a great success, that handsome Prince Charming from England left there, on the lawns, a whole string of enchanted ravished ladies.'

John Timpson once signed off a programme on Radio 4 rather rapidly with: 'That's all for today, Mike Aspel will be here tomorrow morning.' A letter from a listener asked why he thought the general public would be interested in learning when his *gas bill* was about to arrive!

Hoaxes have been perpetrated in the broadcasting world, principally in the world of television. One or two of them are almost legendary and have usually occurred on April Fool's Day.

One which has passed into legend was carefully planned by the *Panorama* team in 1957. This programme has always been respected for the integrity and probity of its reporting so people tended to believe anything Richard Dimbleby cared to tell them. But that year the team decided to play an elaborate April Fool on the nation. Richard Dimbleby introduced a film called *The Swiss Spaghetti Harvest* made by cameraman Charles de Jaegar. In it girls were shown picking long tendrils of spaghetti from trees, while Dimbleby spoke a very serious commentary about the early arrival of the spaghetti crop – delivered in those reverent tones, for which he was famous. The commentary ended, 'Good-night – on this first day of April.' Many people were taken in and the BBC received lots of angry comments. It was generally felt that *Panorama*, so admired for its honesty, had let everyone down. Many people thought it had no right to have a sense of humour. It did teach one useful lesson: never believe everything people tell you – not even when they are on television. Actually, the *Panorama* team were the ones with egg on their face – April Fool jokes must be played before mid-day.

Richard Dimbleby was the centre of another nationwide 'shock-horror' after just two words spoken when he believed he was 'off-mike'. It happened during a broadcast from Germany in 1965. The Queen was touring Germany and one of the most significant events in her itinerary was going to be a visit to the Berlin Wall. This was scheduled to go out at 8.50 p.m. in the evening with a live commentary by Dimbleby. Technical problems had dogged Dimbleby all week and left everyone feeling on edge. Monitors had failed at crucial moments, lines had been broken, nothing had been easy, and a Royal Tour was always a very demanding occasion. A few minutes before the commentary was due to go on the air, contact was lost with London. In six minutes the lines were open again and Dimbleby started his commentary. Then a message was received from London that the programme was not being received. Richard Francis, the Producer, cried out: 'Hold everything. We're not on the air. London isn't getting us.'

'Jesus wept!' Dimbleby exclaimed.

Unfortunately, the wrong message had been given and the whole nation heard Dimbleby utter, what was considered then, a shocking profanity. The comments from public and press were most disapproving, and the BBC had to issue an official apology and Dimbleby himself had also to apologise.

One joke perpetrated by the *Goon Show* underrated people's gullibility. Listeners heard the announcer, Wallace Greenslade, seemingly interrupt the flow of jokes, to say: 'We must apologise for interrupting the programme, but a mysterious light has beeen seen over East Acton. If anyone can identify the object will they please phone the Defence Board – Milthorpe 0205. A little later the announcement was made again, and then a third time the programme was faded and Greenslade made the same announcement. Many people tried to ring the Milthorpe number, only to find that there was no such place, and the BBC switchboard was inundated with calls – some people even claiming they had seen the object. The BBC was forced to issue an official statement, which said: 'Unfortunately, a number of people took the interruptions seriously. We apologised to them when they phoned, and pointed out that it was announced in the *Radio Times* that the programme was a recording.'

Perhaps we should recall here Orson Welles' famous 1938 radio dramatisation in America of H. G. Wells' *War of the Worlds*. The earth, H. G. Wells had imagined, was invaded by beings from outer space. Orson Welles, a young genius in his twenties, who ran his famous Mercury Theatre Company and presented plays on the Columbia Broadcasting System, was responsible for this production which he wished to make as realistic as possible. It was so effective that city dwellers, thinking the Martians had actually landed, panicked. Over a million people tried to flee from their homes creating huge traffic jams and complete chaos. The power of radio and television in the hands of ingenious and imaginative men must be almost limitless.

Returning, however, to royal occasions, before Prince Andrew was born, the BBC set up a mobile studio in front of Buckingham Palace – and because of the late arrival of the Prince it was there for a week. During the night that the Queen had the baby, Godfrey Talbot, the BBC's Court Correspondent, standing-by in the mobile studio, received a telephone call which came from Wichita, Kansas. Thinking it was a hoax, Talbot was rather terse with his answers, being busy with all he had to do for the BBC. He did open the windows of the van so that the caller could hear the crowd cheering and said that everyone was happy that the Queen had had a boy. He then heard, on the other end of the line, a voice saying: 'That was Godfrey Talbot, British Broadcasting's Buck*ham* man.' Then the voice said: 'That was fine, man. You have the thanks of Radio Wichita. You've been on our air for two minutes and we're sure grateful.'

During the time Godfrey Talbot was waiting outside Buckingham Palace for the arrival of Prince Andrew, he was due to receive a decoration. Prince Philip was standing in for the Queen at the ceremony, who, of course, was otherwise engaged. As he pinned on Talbot's decoration he grinned: 'So this is what you have been hanging round our front gate for all this week!'

What sounded like a hoax was one of those broadcasting clangers. In 1984 Kent listeners enjoyed eavesdropping on Terry Wogan who was broadcasting from a parking lot in Los Angeles. The Olympic Games were in full flow and the

transmissions were being taken by Radio 2 from 11 p.m. to
2 a.m. In between Terry's interviews, records were being
played. It is customary for BBC local radio stations to link
up with Radio 2 when they stop broadcasting their own
programmes. One night, Radio Kent's Engineer set the
switches for the Wogan Programme, forgetting that the records were being relayed from London and not L.A., so
listeners, instead of hearing the records, heard all the private chat between Wogan and his guests, instructions to
engineers, research assistants and comments from the producer. It was over an hour and a half before the engineer
could be routed out of bed and rushed to the studio to
rectify the fault.

Cricket seems to lend itself very easily to hoaxes, or perhaps people who enjoy that sport have plenty of time to
plan them. E. W. Swanton was the subject of a great hoax
which was played on him by Colin Cowdrey and Peter
Richardson, who was then captain of Kent. 'Jim' Swanton,
as he is affectionately known, was commentating on a
county game at Tunbridge Wells. Kent were batting, and
Peter Richardson was at the wicket. On a given signal he
joined his fellow batsman in the centre of the crease, and
appeared to have a very grave conversation. He then went
over to the umpire, Bill Copson, the ex-Derbyshire bowler,
who was also in on the joke. The producer was very puzzled
as to what was going on. Bill Copson strolled towards the
commentary box. Jim Swanton endeavoured to keep the
commentary going, and said he thought there must be some
small boys playing near the commentary box, and that
the umpire was coming over to put a stop to it. Instead of
that, Bill looked up at the commentary box, and called out,
'Will you please stop that booming noise up there, it's putting the batsman off. Please stop it at once.' Jim Swanton
was completely flummoxed by this, and his usual fluency
momentarily deserted him. At that moment, Colin Cowdrey, who was also in the box, called back, 'Sorry, Bill, we
couldn't quite hear. Will you repeat that, please?' Bill Copson did just that, and louder, much to the amusement of

the crowd, and the listeners. Jim Swanton's look of amazement soon disappeared from his face when he saw Peter Richardson doubled up with laughter in the middle of the pitch. Jim now realised that a carefully planned hoax had been played on him. He reasserted his authority, and added stiffly, 'Perhaps they could now get on with the game!'

Another hoax was perpetrated on the cricketing fraternity by that delightful character, Bill Frindall – the one the Radio 3 Commentary Team refer to as 'the bearded wonder'. Bill is the man who produces all those incredible facts and figures that so illuminate the cricket commentaries on Radio 3.

At a party in 1972, his hostess challenged him to do his stint in the commentary box dressed as an Arab. If he succeeded the assembled guests would donate money to his favourite charity. Bill accepted the bet, and a real Arab who was a guest at the party lent Bill a genuine costume. The following day, Bill drove to the Kennington Oval in the morning, and parked his car in his usual place. The official in charge tried to stop him saying that the space was reserved for Mr Frindall. Bill was delighted that he had not been recognised, and realised that his hoax was working. He wound down the window of his car and told the official that he had just bought the Oval, and he was at liberty to park where he jolly well liked. He then took pity on the embarrassed official, explained the joke to him and made him promise not to tell.

He then went to the commentary box, seated himself and tried to look as important as possible. When the rest of the commentary team arrived, they looked askance at the robed figure, but didn't like to challenge him as they thought he might be from the World Service. It was only much later his colleagues rumbled him, when play began and it was necessary to supply some cricketing facts in his correct role as statistician – what a pity it was not on television.

4 · *Announcers and Presenters*

Newscasters, quizmasters, game-show or chat-show hosts speak direct to the viewer or listener and are in the front line as far as things going wrong are concerned. Those who are good at presenting programmes or hosting shows make it look so easy and natural – which is part of the job – that the audience is deceived into thinking that it is easy to chatter on. In fact you need to be very alert and disciplined or you are soon in an awful tangle. Many very good entertainers are quite unable to speak fluently and amusingly without having memorised the script.

Most people who 'front' a show are assumed to be presenting to the public their whole personality, though in fact they are doing just what an actor does and quite deliberately exhibiting the appropriate style and behaviour for that particular show. I have certainly found this to be true since I presented the quiz programme *Sale of the Century*. This developed a very stylised form, with the interplay between the quizmaster and the contestants eliminated, which made me appear as a very smooth, fast-talking, authoritarian character. Some people suppose this to be 'the real me' and will often say, when they meet me or see me perform on stage, 'You're quite different from how you appear on television.' In fronting a quiz show, I discovered quite early on that one was not criticised in the press for the way one handled the show, but for one's manner or appearance, or even for the way one spoke or smiled. My reaction is to point out that were I in a drama playing a thief or murderer it would hardly be assumed that this was behaviour natural to me. My hosting of *Sale of the Century* is in some ways a

performance. *Sale of the Century* is recorded without interruptions as if it were a live programme, which is only fair to
the contestants, and I am under great pressure not to make
any mistakes. Usually this results in me appearing very
fluent or smooth which does not always please my critics.
The main thing, however, is that provided the public enjoys
the shows, then the programme is successful.

There was one moment in *Sale of the Century* when I
really felt the egg on my face, since there was nothing I
could do about it at the time, except try and flannel my way
out of it. The situation was made worse in the second half
of the programme, when I had to apologise to the viewers
and draw attention to the mix up. In this programme I
deliver the questions fairly rapidly to give a sense of excitement, and normally make my own decisions as to whether
the answer given is sufficient to give the contestant the
money. As a back-up, the adjudicator of the programme,
who is the head of religious broadcasting at Anglia Television, and the question compiler, David Self, are seated
alongside the producer in the control room watching the
programme as it is being recorded. We have worked out a
signal, where if I am unsure whether the contestant has said
sufficient to warrant the money, I create a small hesitation
with a long drawn out 'well'. During that pause the adjudicator quickly looks at the question compiler, has a quick
word and then rapidly says yes or no to the producer, who
then presses one of two buttons bringing on a red light on
my desk for a refusal and a green light for acceptance. On
this occasion I had awarded the contestant the money, and
then thought I should have confirmation of my decision.
Within seconds the red light was flashing, so I 'flannelled'
about my decision, and said on reflection that I didn't think
the contestant had said sufficient and I would have to take
the money away.

When the recording of the first half was over, the producer requested, via the studio manager, that I should go
and see him in the control room. On arrival, he looked at
me with amazement, 'What are you playing at? You re-

quested confirmation, and we told you to accept.' I said, 'You told me to refuse, the red light came on, and I reversed my decision.' He said, 'I pressed the green light.' I insisted that the red light had come on, so the lights were then checked, and it was discovered that the electrician, on assembling the desk for the recording on that day, had managed to cross the wires, so when the button for the red light was pressed, the green one came on. It was impossible to re-record the first half of the show and I was asked to explain to the viewers in the second half that I was going to reverse my decision. There was not time to explain the technical slip-up – and I doubt the viewers would have understood if I had tried. Can you imagine what it felt like to begin the second half of the recording and have to explain that I was now going to change my mind once again. The situation was not of my making, but it was one of those occasions when the person in front of the camera has to take all the 'flak', and is the one left standing with 'egg on the face'!

Clangers and hiccups don't usually occur in a quiz show, or rather because the general public are involved, anything a contestant says or does in this unrehearsed situation is a natural part of the programme. For instance, when I asked the question, 'What should you do if you live in a glass house?', a female contestant pressed her buzzer and replied, 'Not take a bath.' It received a huge laugh and she blushed deeply. I was sorry I couldn't give her the money for inventiveness.

There have been occasions, however, when I felt I had to protect a contestant from him or herself, since they feel the egg on their face far more deeply than a professional. The question was, 'What is a *billet-doux*?' A female contestant replied, 'It's something you sit on in the bathroom ... er ... you wash yourself on it', then she paused, thinking she might have made a mistake, and I had the delicate task of pointing out to her what she was thinking of was a bidet. The audience laughed, but it was necessary to put the contestant at ease immediately, since on television for the first time it is easy to feel you have made a fool of yourself before millions, and this can be inhibiting and spoil the rest of the show.

Jim Bowen, the presenter of the programme *Bullseye*, tells of the occasion on the programme when he felt the egg well and truly on his face. As he read out the question, he also read out the answer. Such a natural mistake delights an audience and is well worth keeping. A recorded programme can look very dead when all such slips are edited out.

Bob Monkhouse, that master quiz-game host, tells of an occasion when he was presenting *The Golden Shot*. This show went out live. As Bob says, 'That can be very exciting for the performer, but can make a contestant even more nervous at the thought of being viewed instantly by millions.' On this occasion a female contestant must have been more nervous than usual and disappeared into the loo just when she was wanted. Suddenly she heard her name called, jumped to her feet and knocked herself out on the door.

The BBC have also had their embarrassing moments with quiz programmes. It was only the honesty of one man which saved them from having 'egg on the face' with that marvellous programme *Mastermind*. A man who had been accepted as a contestant for this programme, had chosen as his subject on which to answer questions 'The Life and Work of the composer Franz Liszt'. On this programme the specialist questions are prepared by someone well-informed on the subject, so one of the production team telephoned the Liszt Society, and asked them to suggest an expert who would do the job of setting the *Mastermind* questions. 'I don't think you should be asking me,' replied the voice on the other end of the phone, 'I am the person who will be competing in the programme.'

Eamon Andrews is, of course, a true professional and makes it all look deceptively easy. He started as a sports commentator, like a number of well-known presenters and link men, and after moving on to panel games and other shows, he eventually landed the job of presenting *This Is Your Life*, which calls for all of his experience, professional skill and Irish charm. His name is now almost synonymous with the programme but it was not all plain sailing in the early days.

Although it was possible to record the programme, it was felt that it would be more real if it went out live. The producer arranged what was called the 'pick-up' earlier on the day the show went out, and then hurried the 'subject', which is how they describe the unsuspecting victim, over to the studios where he is carefully hidden from all the guests who are going to appear in his 'life' until it is time for transmission.

This system of preparing and transmitting the programme was changed after a pick-up went wrong in a way which the producers obviously thought would never happen. The drama captured the headlines in the newspapers the next day, and cost the BBC – who were then transmitting the programme – a considerable amount of money, and a fair amount of egg on its face. Danny Blanchflower had achieved great success as a footballer, not only captaining Tottenham Hotspur and Northern Ireland, but having the distinction of leading Spurs to the then unique success of what is called 'the Double', winning the League and FA Cup in the same season. He was an ideal choice as a person around whom to build a *This Is Your Life* programme. The year was 1959, and it was decided to organise the pick-up at Broadcasting House, the headquarters of BBC Radio. Danny was invited to come to Broadcasting House in the late afternoon of the day on which the transmission was due to take place and record an interview with Dennis Law and Matt Busby for *Saturday Sportsround*. It gives one some idea of how casual they were in those days when one realises that Danny came up to Broadcasting House on the Tube from his North London home. Nowadays the 'subject' is collected by car and he or she is shepherded carefully by a member of the production team.

Danny, being a punctual person, arrived a little early, and was met by the producer of the sports programme, Angus Mackay, who proceeded to walk him round Broad-

45

casting House on some pretext or other before going up to one of the many small recording studios. Arriving in the studio Danny noticed the television camera but thought this was not unusual since in those days he knew television inserts were sometimes recorded at Broadcasting House. He was a little puzzled by Angus Mackay's behaviour but before he had time to ponder this, Eamon Andrews stepped out from the shadows behind the camera with a book under his arm, approached Danny, and after the usual flowery introduction that one has come to associate with this programme, announced, 'Danny Blanchflower, this is your life.' Danny replied, 'Oh, no, it's not,' and something else which we won't repeat, and promptly left the studio. He remembers hurrying down the stairs, hotly pursued by Eamon Andrews. When Eamon caught up with him he was delighted and said, 'That was wonderful, the best start we have ever had.' Danny replied, 'No it wasn't, because I am not doing the programme.' They were then joined by Angus Mackay, who had rushed out of the studio and down the stairs, falling and hurting his leg as he did so. Danny always remembers the fact that Angus was not apologetic about what had occurred, but cross that he had hurt himself. Danny was then invited by the two of them to go over to the BBC Club, which he agreed to do, although he was adamant he would not go through with the programme. Everyone concerned with the show was in quite a state by now, since they knew that in the TV studio at Lime Grove, there were a large number of friends and well-known guests assembled from all over the country, including the whole of the Spurs Football Team, expecting to take part in Danny Blanchflower's 'life'.

At the BBC Club, Danny was invited to have a double whisky, which Danny refused in favour of a soft drink, leaving the whisky for those who needed it more than him. Eamon Andrews in a final effort to persuade him to change his mind, offered to let him look through the book of his 'life' that had been prepared, to convince him that nothing would occur that was likely to embarrass him, and that it was going to be a happy and enjoyable occasion with his family and friends. What had been overlooked by those who had researched the show was that Danny was a man of principle and he did not enjoy being tricked. Such is the power of television, that those associated with it assume that everyone will come running once it beckons.

Danny could not be persuaded. He was at great pains to point out that he had no reservations about appearing in the programme and was fully aware of the trouble and expense to which the producers had gone in assembling the show, but he had been invited there under false pretences, and as a matter of principle he was not prepared to go through with the programme they had planned. He made his excuses and left to take the Tube back home. Even in those days, a lot of people had difficulty in understanding such firmly held convictions, including some of the press. One of the many journalists who phoned him when the news had leaked even had the effrontery to suggest that he had been in prison and was frightened that this might come up in the programme. Danny, being an intelligent man, and used to handling this type of journalist, joked, 'to which prison sentence are you referring?' Other people thought his decision was an act of retaliation against the BBC against whom he obviously must hold a grudge. None of which was, of course, true. In fact, some years later he was invited to appear on that memorable programme *Face to Face*, in which John Freeman encouraged people to talk very frankly about their life and background. This series is probably best remembered for the famous occasion when the aggressive broadcaster, Gilbert Harding, face to face with Freeman, broke down and cried. Danny agreed to appear in this programme, but when he arrived at the studio, he was informed that they would not be discussing the situation that occurred when he walked out on *This Is Your Life*. Again, Danny's honesty and high principles asserted themselves. He pointed out that he had agreed to take part on the basis that no subject would be barred from discussion. In fact, he threatened to leave if the affair was not

47

brought up, since it not only gave him the opportunity to explain the reasons for his action which he thought had been misrepresented, but also because he suspected that someone in the BBC had requested that the subject should not be discussed. No doubt there were those in the Corporation who still felt the 'egg on their faces' as a result of Danny's action on that occasion.

As a result of Danny Blanchflower walking out of *This Is Your Life* someone else had egg on their face. As already mentioned, the whole of the Spurs team were invited to be guests on the programme, but like all guests they were sworn to secrecy for fear the news would leak to the person who was the 'subject' of the show. The Spurs' goal-keeper, Bill Brown, a good friend of Danny's, was asked by his wife as he left home that evening, where he was going. Not wishing to tell a lie, he said that he was unable to tell her, but if she looked at the television during the evening all would be revealed. When Danny didn't turn up at Lime Grove studios that evening the BBC were forced to substitute a recording of a past *This Is Your Life*. Everyone who had assembled to take part in Danny's 'life' was not only disappointed that the programme was not going to take place, but rather fed up after making the journey to the studio and giving up an evening to it. Also, some people had been flown in at the BBC's expense from abroad. In the circumstances all the BBC could do was to invite everyone present to the party which normally followed the show, but on this occasion without the 'subject'. One can imagine that the atmosphere was a bit flat, and perhaps some of them tried to forget their disappointment in the free refreshments being offered. Anyway, some time later Bill Brown set off in his car for his home in North London, having forgotten what he had told his wife. She had switched on the television, deducing that his reason for secrecy could only be concerned with the *This Is Your Life* programme which was on that night. She saw a programme about someone's life that had nothing to do with her husband and unfortunately on his way home Bill's car broke down, with the result that he arrived back very late. Bill's wife was naturally very suspicious, and it was some time before Bill could convince her of the truth of his story.

As a result of Danny Blanchflower's action, *This Is Your Life* very soon stopped going out live. These days, Thames Television, who now produce the show, record it about two weeks in advance. They don't like to have a longer gap, for fear that news of the recording might get around, and the programme lose some of its impact. The two-week gap means they have always one programme in hand, so if any 'subject' decided that he or she did not wish to go through with the show, they are not left with an embarrassing space in the schedules. Also, recording the programme gives the producer the chance to trim any particular item, should the guest overrun his or her allotted time, which makes the programme look very slick.

I have had the pleasure of being the 'subject' on *This Is Your Life*. In retrospect it turned out to be hilarious, and for the production team, a very 'hairy' time. This was due in part to the fact that the executive producer at Thames Television is extremely careful to ensure that there are no leaks and the 'subject' remains unsuspecting. In fact, in order to achieve maximum security, not only is the programme transmitted two weeks after being filmed but also the subject's friends are only invited two weeks before the filming. Getting everyone together in such a short time is quite an achievement when you consider that the programme's researchers have to track down relations or friends of the 'subject' who might be in another country, and for whom they may not even have an address.

Secrets are not easy to keep even for a fortnight. After it was over, my wife, daughter, son, agent and others closely involved, told me that they all felt they dropped a clanger at some point. They had all said or done something which did not ring true, and expected me to guess what was afoot. If, however, you are not looking for anything unusual, any 'cover-up' remark made to you is accepted as a genuine statement of fact. The producers make such efforts to eli-

minate the possibility of the 'subject' becoming suspicious
during the 'pick-up', that they almost trip themselves up in
their conscientiousness. This certainly happened in the
pick-up they organised for me. My Press Agent, Margo
Lovell, had some time previously arranged for me to give
an interview to a magazine for an article they were putting
together about cricket teas. I had to have some photographs
taken for this at the Oval. About a week before this was due
to happen, I was told that a number of other well-known
names in the entertainment and cricket world were also
going to be at the Oval to be photographed for the article.
The fact they were all personal friends of mine didn't make
me in the least suspicious. Thames Television had decided
it would be a good idea for the programme to film me at
the Oval, after the magazine's photographer had finished.
Then I would be lured to a pick-up point and Thames
would film the others in my absence talking about my love
of cricket and my involvement in the Lord's Taverners'
charity work. I heard afterwards that Margo Lovell had
suggested that the Oval would be an ideal venue for the
pick-up but Thames vetoed the idea since I might see the
television recording van on arrival and become suspicious.
So it was decided that the pick-up should take place at the
White House Hotel, and Anne Knight, a partner in my
agent's office, agreed to be involved. She told me on the
telephone that an American impresario was interested in
talking to me about a job on television in the States. This
rang true, since *Sale of the Century* was a programme ori-
ginating in America, and I had appeared in a situation comedy series on American television. Anne Knight said that
she would accompany me to the meeting, which sounded
potentially very exciting. This is where things began to go
slightly wrong for Thames. I placed so much importance
on the outcome of this meeting with the American producer
that I telephoned Margo and asked her to get me out of the
photographic session at the Oval. I can imagine how the
lines must have been buzzing between her and the production team of *This Is Your Life*. When she came back on the

phone and said that it was going to be difficult, I pointed out that they had a lot of people for the photograph so they would not miss me. Also, I said, it was very important that I was not late for the appointment at the White House Hotel, and it would be cutting things very fine to get there by six o'clock. The telephone lines buzzed again, and the producer of *This Is Your Life* thought up another ploy. Margo was soon back on the phone to me saying that Thames had decided to cover the photographic session and would actually interview me for a sports programme talking about cricket. This was clever, since here was something that really appealed to me. I was, however, still worried that I would not make my appointment with the American. Again the lines buzzed. Again, Margo was back on the phone to me: 'Thames Television,' she assured me, 'are so keen for you to do this interview, they will supply a car to take you from your home to the Oval, wait there and be available to take you to your appointment at the hotel, and will guarantee that you are not late.' The situation had been salvaged and it would not matter now if I saw the television recording van at the Oval. These preparations, which to some might seem over elaborate, nearly floundered again.

On the day of the Oval interviews and my meeting with the American television executive, it so happened that a representative from BBC Television came to my house to discuss my appearance in a programme series they were producing. This was something very important to me since I didn't work a great deal for the BBC and was therefore keen to take part in the series. The discussions took place in the early afternoon and went very well. The researcher from the BBC was still asking questions and I was still talking when the hire-car from Thames Television arrived to take me to the Oval. I asked the driver to wait a few minutes while I finished the interview. He seemed rather agitated and came back to the house a few minutes later and said it was important that we left to keep the appointment. This struck me as unusual, since drivers of hire-cars don't usually know the details or one's business. I told

him that it was not important since the event at the Oval
was primarily an occasion for press photographs to be taken
and, since there were already a number of well-known
people there, it probably wouldn't matter if I was late. The
poor man was in somewhat of a panic now, and I was told
later he went back to his car and broadcast on the car radio
to his employers that he could not get the 'subject' out of
his house! He was told to go back on some excuse and say
firmly that Thames Television had requested that I should
be there, and find some way of making me leave immediately. A little later, we were driving at breakneck speed
from north London to the Oval, south of the river. On
arrival I quickly changed into my cricket clothes as requested, and joined the others who were already in cricket
gear standing around a large table magnificently laid out
with the most sumptuous Cricket Tea you ever saw. It was
most appetizing. The photographs were taken. The magazine was delighted, then the producer of the television film
unit said, 'Now Nicholas, I know you have to be away for
an important appointment, so can we quickly record your
interview for our sports programme.' A Thames sports
commentator had arrived for my 'interview' and in no time
the cameras were rolling. Actually, all the technicians were
acting and nothing was being recorded. I remember being
thrown off balance by the first question that I was given in
this phoney interview, since it was far too provocative: 'Do
you think that Geoff Boycott or Mike Brierley should captain England?' I flannelled away on the basis that this was
not a good question to put to a cricket enthusiast since I
didn't wish to be involved in the politics of the game. I just
stressed the cricketing ability of both men. I was certainly
thrown by the question since I thought I was going to be
interviewed about my personal interest and approach to the
game. The interview was soon over – I was told they didn't
require a great deal – and it was suggested that I hurry
upstairs and change so as not to be late for my next appointment. This I did, but once again, the whole secret was
nearly blown, and the producer told me afterwards that he

thought I had guessed and blamed himself for not being more careful.

What happened was this: after I went to change, they began the genuine filming of comments from the others about me, which was to be included in the actual programme later that evening. In packing up my cricket things, I discovered that I had left my sweater in the room where the filming was taking place. On my way downstairs to the waiting car, I walked into this room to collect my sweater. I remember the moment to this day. As I entered there was an instant silence in which you could almost hear a bail drop. They had been in the middle of filming, and one of my friends had just recorded a remark about me. Everyone assumed that I had heard this, and stood about nervously awaiting some remark from me. Not having heard anything I assumed that I had walked in while the camera was running – which was true – and they were filming a silent shot, so I mimed to everyone that I had forgotten something, and tiptoed across the room, picked up my sweater from where I had left it, and tiptoed out waving my goodbyes. I must have looked even more foolish than I felt. The secret, however, was still intact. I hurried to the waiting car, and we then set out for the hotel. I remember being puzzled by the route that the driver was taking, which was due to the fact that he realised he had time in hand, and did not wish to deliver me too early for the appointment. Since I know London very well from driving a great deal, I suggested that there was a quicker route than the one he was taking. He was at pains to defend the roundabout way he was going, but again no thought that anything unusual or underhand was going on crossed my mind – why should it? I just assumed the driver was a bit of a dunce when it came to knowing his way around London. I arrived at the hotel, was greeted by Anne Knight, who suggested that we might go to the bar and have a drink. This was to be the spot where the actual pick-up was going to take place. Anne Knight was going to call for the barman, and Eamon Andrews was going to pop up from behind the bar, with the book under his arm, and greet me in his normal way and inform me that, 'This Is Your Life'. Apparently, we were still a little early, and as we walked into the cocktail bar, I noticed two of the girls who had appeared with me on *Sale of the Century*. They were, of course, to be part of the programme. As I hadn't seen either of the girls for a year or two I said to Anne, 'Oh, there's Linda. Let's go over and say hello; I haven't seen her for ages.' Anne Knight, who was by nature a very gentle person, then did something utterly uncharacteristic, which at the time I couldn't understand. She had been given instructions to steer me to a certain point at the bar and this she was determined to do. I had not been supposed to see the girls and certainly it would ruin everything if I went and talked to them. Poor Anne in a state of mild panic grabbed me aggressively by the arm and said, 'Oh, no you're not. You're going to have a drink with *me*,' and forcibly propelled me to the required position at the bar. Before I had time to think about this, Eamon was doing his stuff and all was made clear. To me it was one of the most exciting and memorable evenings of my life. In what other circumstances could one have such a marvellous surprise party, with so many relatives and friends all brought together at someone else's expense!

Judith Chalmers is one of the most professional presenters in this country. Equally at home on radio or television, she has covered nearly every kind of event. She appears regularly on the Thames Television holiday programme, *Wish You Were Here*, in which she had one of her most embarrassing experiences. Fortunately it occurred in the age of recorded television programmes so neither she nor the director experienced the egg that would have been on their faces had it been transmitted.

Judith was scheduled to go up to Scotland to film a sequence for the programme. This holiday covered a trip from Fort William, via Mallaig, up to the Isles of Skye. The director and the writer for the programme went up a day in advance to do a reconnaissance, and find the best places in which to film. Judith arrived with the film crew.

They were joined by the director and the writer, and they all boarded the train at Fort William. They went to the observation car on the train, from where they were going to film. The observation car is a specially designed carriage, which gives its occupants a splendid view of the scenery outside. Judith had been given her script which she had memorised. The director had worked out the precise moment at which he wished to begin filming, in order to have the best scenery in the background, magnificent mountains and heather. As this moment approached, the carriage became very steamed up. There was not only the normal complement of passengers, one of whom was Judith, but also the film crew, so there were a large number of people in a small area. The director told them to 'stand by', so the assistant cleaned the steam off the windows. The sound engineer put the microphone on Judith and confirmed everything was in working order. The lighting engineer put on all his lights. The cameraman indicated he was ready to go. The director said, 'Action', and the train went straight into a tunnel! The pay-off occurred a few minutes later. Everything was set up to start filming again. They went through the same procedures, and as the director said, 'Action', the train went into another tunnel. When they emerged into daylight the other side of the tunnel, there were only a few minutes left before the train reached Mallaig. It was imperative they had this opening shot in the can on this part of the journey. The background scenery now became secondary. The camera crew quickly set up, and Judith being a true professional didn't fluff her lines, and they did the opening shot in one take. It was a long time before the director lived that one down: they all wanted to know what he had been doing on his reconnaissance!

Those who read the news are in many ways a rather special breed of person. They hold a unique and somewhat privileged position in our modern society, and perform a task which requires very special skills to do well, and if they are successful they achieve a popularity which is quite astounding.

When one thinks of the style and charm of some of our best newsreaders, I am always impressed with how deceptively easy they make it look. It is only when you see a bad newsreader you realise how professional the good ones are. A newsreader must be authoritative, informative, appear relaxed and have no irritating vocal mannerisms. He or she must project a pleasant personality but never convey sympathy with any one point of view. At the same time, there are technical requirements of which they have to be aware, such as the time factor, pronunciation and possible signals from the producer via the studio manager. If there is a hiccup and something goes wrong, or if a sentence is read incorrectly or a word wrongly pronounced the newsreader will look more foolish, or have more egg on his face, than would occur in any other programme.

Robert Dougall, the doyen of newsreaders for so long but now retired, has recalled his experiences. Originally he was an announcer on BBC sound radio but began reading the news on television shortly after the War. He remembers how difficult it was to learn the new techniques and skills required for television newscasting, especially as in those days they didn't have the technical back-up, such as the sophisticated autocue that exists today. The production staff and editors were learning as they went along how best to present news programmes. Robert Dougall admits that it was on occasions a nightmarish business, as everyone involved struggled to find an interesting and appealing way to make the news visually interesting. For instance, the sub-editors had to learn to write their scripts to fit a section of film, which meant acquiring the discipline of writing with a stop-watch. It was estimated that newscasters would read at the rate of about three words per second. Newsreaders had to become more like actors. No longer were they unseen voices delivering their information in well-modulated tones. They were visible and their expressions would be interpreted by the viewer. They had to catch the mood of a story without appearing to be involved in it. For the first time they were having to learn to vary their pace and pitch without making their reading overdramatic. Robert says that some of the early newsreaders never fully learnt how to cope with speaking alongside filmed reports, and quotes one in particular who was so set in his ways that his deliberately modulated tones were time and again to be heard meandering on long after the appropriate section of film had ceased. He would, for instance, still be reading an account of a *grand prix* motor race while the picture on the screen showed a funeral. One evening, a senior editor, driven to distraction, stood behind the said newsreader's chair, and whenever his commentary overran the film the editor clamped his hand firmly over the reader's mouth.

In 1957 Robert Dougall had a very awkward moment. He had to do a commentary on a series of natural disasters round the world – a forest fire in Canada, avalanches in Austria and some floods elsewhere. The script had somehow got into the wrong sequence and while Bob was describing one event, another came on to the screen. Words and pictures were definitely *not* synchronised. Deciding that the situation was impossible Bob broke off and said, 'I am so sorry but as you can see we have got our elements mixed.'

Those telephones which ring occasionally during a bulletin generally tell a newscaster not to read an item, or that a piece of film hasn't yet arrived and so the item must be put last and so on. But on one occasion Dougall's telephone rang, he picked it up and found no one at the other end. Rather than give the game away he listened to the silence for a moment, then said, 'I see – thank you very much' and put the receiver down.

Michael Aspel, when he was reading the news on one occasion, heard his telephone ring but couldn't find it. The cleaner had safely stowed it away in a desk drawer.

One of the greatest commentators and presenters of all time was the late Richard Dimbleby. In fact, he can claim to have practically invented the job. Before he came on to the scene, BBC radio used to take reports from the news agencies and were often behind the daily newspapers with the news – something that seems incredible nowadays. It was during the War when Dimbleby's often controversial reports from the Middle East caused such a stir. Thanks to Dimbleby, vivid reporting, such as we have today, became a reality. In fact, so controversial were some of his reports and so expensive (in BBC terms) was his lifestyle that Dimbleby was recalled from the Middle East. But this did not stop him. Here is his son, Jonathan's account of one of Richard Dimbleby's exploits:

'On 6 January (1943) he became the first BBC war correspondent to go on an RAF bombing raid. He looked forward to the mission with Bomber Command with no excitement and considerable fear. He was to fly with Guy Gibson in a Lancaster bomber and their destination was Berlin. It was a night raid, and as they roared along the runway and took off, he counted around him between thirty and forty bombers: "seemingly suspended in the evening air". As they climbed over the south coast, above the cloud, he switched on his oxygen supply. He felt nervous and tired. And then drowsy. He fell asleep. The next moment he was lying semi-conscious on the floor of the plane, with the co-pilot bending anxiously over him, fiddling with his oxygen mask. He had nipped the tube of oxygen supply and knocked himself out. It did not seem an auspicious beginning.'

Dimbleby survived giving a fluent and brilliant description of what it was like to be aloft during a bombing raid. He was the true professional, chronicling actual events, telling people at home 'how it was'. But he paid the penalty for his efforts coming back. Exhaustion, the twisting and turning of the bomber and his justified fear overcame him. He turned away from Gibson and vomited on the floor beside him, just missing the bomb-aimer.

In 1952 French and British television decided to hold a joint *Grande Semaine de Paris* – it was the first occasion a joint production had been planned. The programmes from Paris were supposed to show the beauties and magnificence of that city, and give some idea of life there. Richard Dim-

HIMMEL GOTT! IF WE EFFER
HAF A THOUSAND DIMBLEBY RAID!

bleby as the top BBC presenter and commentator, was sent over to cover the event. The French TV personnel, however, showed, to quote Jonathan Dimbleby, 'A level of enthusiastic incompetence and chauvinistic arrogance that their BBC guests had not thought possible!' The broadcasts were not made any easier by a ferocious thunderstorm on the first night, Dimbleby was heard to say: 'The combined forces of the BBC and the French Television Service can't beat the weather.'

Worse was to follow. A night out in Paris had been planned as one programme, and it was decided that this should take place on one of the celebrated *bateaux mouches* which chug up and down the Seine. But because three cameras would be needed to transmit the programme, it was decided that the *bateau mouche* would be moored beside the riverbank. One of the artists engaged to appear was Line Renou, a popular singer in Paris at that time. Mademoiselle Renou had pre-recorded her song and was to mime it to the music. On cue, she stood up and started to mime the words – there was silence. The play-back machine had broken down. Dimbleby, the anchor man, invited the singer to sit down, and started the interview again. The director signalled that all was well, Line Renou went to take her place, then the camera packed up! '*Mon Dieu!*' shrieked the director and ran across the set and started to scream at the English crew, who understood not a word of his voluble French. The floor manager (Stephen McCormack) decided to take over, and with the camera which was working, he and Dimbleby started to do a tour of the boat – all completely unrehearsed – but in London it was decided that enough was enough and the plugs were pulled! Dimbleby was very angry, picked up a bottle of champagne, held it aloft and threw it into the Seine. He did it again with a second bottle. Then he left the boat, exclaiming, 'I will never, God help me, work with those clots again.'

Gilbert Harding was well known for his caustic and peppery temper. He was not, therefore, an ideal interviewer as he certainly didn't suffer fools gladly and could become very sarcastic if he received what he considered stupid answers. He was, however, sometimes used in this capacity, and in one programme, in a market town he stopped a man, as instructed, and truculently enquired. 'What are you?' The man, resenting his tone, answered, 'What's that got to do with you?' 'I'm from the BBC', said Harding tersely. 'Oh, well, then,' said the man, 'I suppose I'd better tell you. I'm a gentleman farmer.' 'Impossible,' said Harding, 'you can't be both!'

Television announcers face another hazard. People they never meet or have ever heard of 'fall in love' with their image on the screen. Donald Gray, for instance, who began as an actor and became an announcer in the early days of television was extremely good-looking with a most attractive speaking voice. Viewers thought he was wonderful and he was once threatened by a jealous husband whose wife used to kiss the screen every time he appeared.

As a commentator, it is sometimes difficult not to slip up while keeping the commentary flowing, especially if one is describing somewhat mundane events. That excellent commentator, Wynford Vaughan Thomas, who has the Welsh gift for speaking fluently and choosing just the right phrase, was describing what went on in a steel works and, as a white-hot rod of steel passed him, was heard to say, 'Here comes thirty foot of white-hot steel, untouched by human hand!'

Even on radio when doing a commentary, it must be a challenge on occasions to think of something interesting or original to say, especially when one has been covering a long event. Tom Fleming, during a programme covering the Royal Jubilee, was heard to say, 'One wonders what the conversation will be in the stable tonight when these horses get home.'

The commentator on the World Snooker Championships in 1983 was struggling to find something different to say as the camera panned over Jimmy White, the top snooker player, sitting rather tense during a long break by his opponent. In the hushed tones that a commentator uses during a snooker game, he remarked, 'There is Jimmy looking very pale, but then his name is White.'

You never know what is going to happen on a live show, even on radio. Michael Standing was probably best known for his programme *Standing on the Corner*, in which he used to stand literally on a corner and comment on events. On one occasion he was describing the Ceremony of the Keys at the Tower of London, and finished by saying, 'and now silence descends on Tower Hill'. At that precise moment half a dozen motor bikes appeared from nowhere and set up the most infernal din.

On radio, announcers can be made to feel foolish when the phraseology of what they have to deliver hasn't been well thought through. On Capital Radio recently an announcer found himself saying, 'Cat owners are advised to put a collar on their cats – dog owners too – so that the authorities can know the difference.'

Another hazard for announcers on radio or television which can make them feel they have 'egg on the face', occurs when the wrong piece of paper is passed to them. In January 1985 a BBC radio announcer after reading the news, said, 'Here again are the news headlines. Princess Margaret has had an operation for the removal of a small part of her left lung . . . I am sorry about that . . . wrong cue . . . Christopher Columbus was not the first man to reach the Americas. . .'

It was soon obvious in the March 1966 General Election that the Labour Party was being returned to office and that Harold Wilson would remain Prime Minister. The BBC and ITV had arranged to bring him back from Huyton, his constituency, to Euston in a special train at their joint expense. They both wanted to interview him, and transmit the programme as soon as possible, from the train itself. John Morgan, the BBC interviewer, was prepared with his questions but at that time Wilson was not best pleased with the BBC, and he refused to be interviewed by their representative and quite a row broke out. Wilson then gave a very long interview to ITV.

It was left to Desmond Wilcox to redeem the situation

for the BBC. He had been on duty most of the night and was at Euston Station talking to commuters, and longing to go home. He received a call from Paul Fox, masterminding the election coverage for the BBC. Cautioning Desmond to be careful in what he said, Fox asked him if he would try to get an interview with Wilson. Fox went on, 'You've only been with the BBC a few weeks, and Harold Wilson knows you well from all the times you've interviewed him on *This Week*. He may not even know you've crossed over – take your BBC pass out of your lapel and stand away from any BBC equipment.' Fox also explained about the row. John Morgan was told not to greet Desmond, and when the train drew in Desmond tore along the platform and persuaded the Prime Minister to give his interview, spending seven minutes with him.

Years later Desmond Wilcox told Harold Wilson what had happened and asked him if he had known that the interview was for the BBC. Wilson replied: 'Ah, you don't think that I'd be daft enough ever to confirm that you and Paul Fox had put one over on me, now do you?'

Many things can affect the weather and now and again the rain rains when the forecast was sun and *vice versa*, and the TV weather men come in for more than their fair share of criticism. There are, however, other more down to earth problems when your job is always done 'live'. In earlier days at the BBC, the weather forecast was of indeterminate length, rounding off the *News* so that the next programme would start on time. Often the weather man didn't know the 'out-time' until the moment he started, and to assist him in finishing on time, the assistant floor manager stood by a pedestal clock beside the camera with a finger on the second when the forecaster had to stop. Jack Scott, the well-known weather forecaster, had developed a habit of winking at the assistant floor manager in appreciation, the moment they were off the air. He was a little worried one evening to notice on the monitor that his broad wink had been transmitted. He need not have worried; there was no reaction from his Masters.

About a week later, however, Richard Baker came to him, puzzled, with a letter he had received from a little girl. 'Dear Mr Baker', she had written, 'Tonight you said "that's the end of the News; now here's the weather from Jack Scott." You should know, Mr Baker, that Jack Scott doesn't give us the weather, God does. And what's more, Jack Scott seemed to know, because he winked at you at the end!'

Richard Kershaw is a very experienced and professional presenter and interviewer on current affairs programmes. In 1976 he was co-presenter with Robin Day of the BBC 2 programme *News Day*. He was interviewing Sir Alan Marre, the first Ombudsman, on his retirement at the end of his term of office. Richard wanted to ask Sir Alan whether he felt restricted by the limited powers he had been given. It was a live show and the word he searched for was circumscribed, but unfortunately the question came out as follows, 'Sir Alan, do you feel circumcised by your restricted powers?' Robin Day, sitting close by, tried desperately to suppress a laugh. Sir Alan Marre was either very professional or never realised the wrong word had been used. He replied simply, 'You could put it that way. My powers are somewhat limited.' The most surprising thing about this incident is that nobody wrote in to complain or even comment, which only proves that if you say something with complete confidence and authority you can get away with almost anything.

Barry Norman, who presents the film review programme on BBC television with such style and eloquence, occasionally does a programme in his series devoted entirely to one artist. In 1974 they had planned a thirty-minute special about Richard Burton. Barry had flown with the film crew to Milan, where Burton was filming, in order to interview him for this particular programme. It had been arranged to film this interview in Burton's hotel suite. The camera was set up, the film crew were standing by, Barry Norman was comfortably seated in one chair, and Richard Burton was casually lounging in another. Unfortunately for Barry, Burton was going through a very emotional phase of his life. He had recently been reconciled with Elizabeth Taylor who at that moment was unwell and stranded in Rome, and he was filming with Sophia Loren, and unable to get away from Milan to join her. By the time he arrived for the recording it seemed he had been drinking to help cope with the stress and strain he was obviously feeling.

The interview began, and was going quite smoothly, and Barry was putting his fourth question, when he heard snoring coming from Richard Burton. Barry looked across at him to discover he was fast asleep. He felt most embarrassed and rather foolish, and did the obvious thing – he asked Burton if he would wake up. He received no response, only more snoring. Barry, realising it was only a recording and could be edited, nudged Burton more firmly, and asked more loudly if he would wake up and continue the interview. Again Barry received no response, so he looked at the director and shrugged. The director looked at Barry and shrugged. The cameraman looked at Barry and shrugged. Then, with a nod from the director the camera was switched off. The equipment was packed away, and not exactly silently, all the crew and Barry Norman left the hotel suite. Throughout all this Richard Burton remained in a comatose state, gently snoring to himself. The following morning Richard Burton had no recollection of the incident, and another day had to be found to do the interview. Barry feels that the most embarrassing part of the whole episode was explaining to Richard Burton the following morning why they were unable to continue with the interview that night.

Tony Barton, before he became a disc jockey on Radio 1 and then Radio 2, was a DJ on Radio Luxembourg. This was one of his first Radio engagements and in 1966 he had an experience which he said added years to his life. As all record programmes on radio are live, it was only his quick thinking and his incredibly quick actions in a potentially disastrous situation that prevented him – and the whole of Radio Luxembourg – having 'Egg on their collective face'. One of the engineers at this radio station had particularly horrendous memories of how the Gestapo had treated his brother on Christmas Day. For this reason he hated Christmas, and whenever December the 25th came around distressing memories would come flooding back to haunt him. It so happened that he had been scheduled to be on duty on Christmas Day in 1966, when Tony was doing his programme. He had arrived during the day with a briefcase of sandwiches but looking very pale and drawn.

In spite of this he appeared to be fulfilling his duties quite adequately, even if he wasn't very coherent which, of course, is not important to an engineer. Tony's programme had been going quite smoothly, and he had reached the moment right at the end when he did a trailer for the programme that was to follow. He introduced his final record, which was duly faded in, and then he casually looked around the studio through the glass panel to where the engineer usually sat and saw there was no one there. He rushed through the communicating door, and there was the engineer lying unconscious in a heap on the floor. Tony knew that he had exactly three minutes before the record on the turntable finished. He rushed down the corridor, grabbed some more records, rushed back, grabbed an engineer from the next door studio, phoned the station manager to warn him of what had happened, rushed back into the studio, switched on, and panting into the microphone – which must have surprised the listeners – he announced that the advertised programme had been changed at the last minute due to an unforeseen technical hitch, and he was going to play some more records. The day was saved!

The cricketer, Tony Lewis, who now writes on the game and presents *Sport On 4*, on the radio, was for a time one of the presenters on *Saturday Night At The Mill*, the late-night talk show, which was transmitted by the BBC live from their Pebble Mill studios in Birmingham. Any live talk show has in-built hazards. On one occasion Tony was scheduled to interview the film actor, Oliver Reed. When they met for a preliminary discussion an hour or two before the transmission, Oliver said there were only two subjects he wished to talk about: his Scottish ancestry and dyslexia. He also objected to the jacket Tony was wearing. Presumably Oliver thought he might wear it on transmission, whereas Tony always presented the show in a dinner-jacket.

Hospitality was provided for everyone, and the time came for the show to begin. Oliver Reed was the final guest. Tony introduced him as one of this country's most exciting stars, and Oliver entered to great applause, with a jacket over his arm, which he insisted Tony put on. Tony was prepared to change his jacket, but then for some reason Oliver pulled out a shirt concealed in his trousers, and wanted Tony to wear this. Then to the amazement of the audience, and in full view of the cameras, Oliver took off his trousers. Tony's mind raced. What was he to do? Would Oliver go further? How could he interview a man in his shirt and underpants? With great skill he manoeuvred Oliver on to the subject of his Scottish ancestry, and said he obviously felt at home with his knees bare, as he must be used to wearing a kilt. This certainly sparked Oliver off – but not in the way Tony expected. Oliver turned to Kenny Ball, whose band played throughout the show, and asked for a Scottish Reel. Kenny and his Jazz Men responded immediately, whereupon Oliver grabbed Tony and tried to dance. Tony had two problems now, to get Oliver seated, but not to allow him to turn either of them as Tony's neck microphone was wired up behind him, and might become disconnected, and then the sound on the show would disappear. Oliver Reed is a very strong man but Tony is no chicken. He managed to keep Oliver facing him, and fortunately Kenny soon stopped playing, so they sat down. Tony admits that inspiration had now failed him, and all he could think of to say was, 'I think we'll cut to the film clip.' While this was showing, hurried messages were passed to Tony that they were running out of time. After the clip there was about two minutes for 'chat', and then he was to cue-in Kenny Ball with the final number.

The film clip finished, and Tony thought it might be a good idea to persuade Oliver Reed to talk about Glenda Jackson, as he knew Oliver admired her very much. This worked very well, and Oliver waxed almost lyrical about her ability and talent, but in a very low key, almost lugubrious voice. Tony was wondering how he could interrupt this sincere tribute to a fine actress and cue-in the now rather inappropriate 'Black Bottom Stomp', the finale music. The floor manager started to give the countdown for the cue to finish. He had reached the point where his ten fingers went up, and he dropped them one by one to indicate the final seconds. Oliver Reed, great professional that he is, had obviously spotted this out of the corner of his eye, and probably realising they needed a high note on which to finish leant forward with five seconds to go and said, 'I'll tell you something else about Glenda Jackson, she has fantastic knockers.' The audience roared, Tony cued the band, the interview was saved. After the finale music, Oliver, still in his shirt and underpants, completely unselfconscious, congratulated Tony on his professional handling of the interview.

5 · Sport

The world of sport is a wonderful area in broadcasting for clangers and hiccups. First of all, nearly all sport goes out 'live'. This is part of the excitement – you are seeing or hearing it as it happens. Even those sporting events which are recorded are treated by everyone concerned with the production, including the commentator, as a live show, since it is unlikely it will be edited before transmission – and even if it is, the verbal clangers cannot always be eliminated. The discipline required of a sports commentator varies according to the sport he is covering and the medium on which it is being broadcast. On radio it is necessary to keep commenting all the time on everything that is going on whereas on television a sport such as tennis or snooker is usually left without commentary while play is in progress. With certain sports such as football and horse racing, the viewer requires more information, and it helps to sustain the excitement to have a 'voice-over'. The brief for any sports commentator is to be interesting, informative and, at whatever pace they are commenting, to convey the excitement of the event. In these circumstances, one can see how easily mistakes can occur, especially verbal ones.

When the pressure is on and the excitement is building the commentator becomes very involved and wouldn't be human if a clanger was not dropped now and then, especially as most sports are concerned with balls. Then there are the strange words and phrases used to describe the actions of the players, the similes and metaphors that spring into the commentator's mind. These are all hazards for the

71

luckless commentator, as are the odd names they give to the positions occupied by players in certain sports. An example of the kind of thing to which I am referring was recounted to me by that well-known sports commentator, Peter West. Peter recalls hearing a Wimbledon commentator on the Centre Court explain, 'Rod Laver will now serve with the Royal balls from the new Box end.'

Private Eye run a column in which verbal clangers, or simply verbal non-sequiturs, are listed under the title of 'Coleman Balls'. David Coleman, who is a splendid sports commentator, has given his name to this column because it is alleged he has made more of these errors than any other commentator. I am sure that isn't true, and he is a great sport the way that he accepts the imputation. In fact, David told me that the column and its title were created following a classic remark made about a long-legged Cuban runner, 'Here comes Juantorena now – every time he opens his legs he shows his class.' Some time after the event, David arranged to have the original tape played back, and it was discovered that the remark had been made by Ron Pickering. It must be very galling to have given your name to a column of verbal clangers, when the original on which it was based had nothing to do with you.

This is not to say that David has not dropped some delightful clangers on occasions, such as, 'Don't tell those coming in the final result of that fantastic match, but let's just have another look at Italy's winning goal.'

Other clangers attributed to David Coleman, which have been enjoyed over the years include:

Of a runner – 'This man could be a dark horse.'

Of a short runner – 'He's even smaller in real life than he is on the track.'

Of a favourite who wasn't doing very well – 'He just can't believe what's not happening to him.'

About Manchester United – 'They are buzzing around the goalmouth like a lot of red blue-bottles.'

Alan Parry, who does football commentaries, is credited with several unfortunate comments, such as:

'. . . and that goal gives him his eleventh goal of the season so far – exactly double what he scored last year!'

'With the last kick of the game, Bobby McDonald scored a header!'

It is very easy to make these slip-ups under pressure. I personally enjoyed the remark of a football commentator, who said, '. . . and I felt a lump in my throat as the ball went in!'

Steve Ryder, the sports presenter, said on Thames Television, in commenting on Pat Jennings, the goalkeeper of Spurs and Northern Ireland, 'His hands are so large, from his thumb to his fingertips is a foot.'

John Snagge, that much-venerated announcer and boat-race commentator, made one of the best known mistakes during the 1949 University race, when he said:

'. . . it's a very close race. I can't see who is in the lead, it is either Oxford or Cambridge.'

John Snagge on another occasion covering the boat-race, said of an Australian Blue:

'He's the only overseas blue rowing in both boats!'

John Snagge was the BBC's senior radio announcer for many years. He had an impeccable delivery and a most beautiful speaking voice. If he made a mistake, it always sounded more unusual than if it had come from a lesser mortal. I remember one occasion when he was reading the news, and said:

'Yorkshire 232 all out, Hutton ill. I am sorry. Hutton 111.'

A commentator with great style and personality in his voice is Brian Johnston. For this reason, it seems more amusing when he makes a mistake, or says something that doesn't quite make sense than when less distinguished commentators drop bricks, like the remark he made at a cricket match between Northampton and Worcester:

'. . . a very disappointing crowd. In fact, I would say that there are more cars here than people.'

Equally, one enjoys it when Brian's remarks have an unintentional double-meaning. During a Test Match between

England and New Zealand in 1969 Alan Ward bowled his fifth ball of the over to Glenn Turner, hitting Turner right on his protective box. Turner's bat flew out of his hand, and he collapsed on the ground writhing in agony. Brian continued describing the scene without explaining where Turner had been hit, not wishing to ruffle the sensibilities of the viewers, though the TV cameras were showing Turner in great discomfort and clutching his vulnerable area. When Turner got up and was given his bat, Brian then continued the commentary as follows:

'. . . it looks as if he's going to try and continue, although he still looks very shaken and pale. Very plucky of him. Yes, he's going to have a try. One ball left!'

A classic clanger was made by an unknown commentator at Henley Royal Regatta. Perhaps, for his sake, it is as well that he remains unknown. Can you imagine the egg that must have been on his face when he said:

'Lady Margaret and Jesus are rowing neck and neck . . . but no, Jesus is now making water in Lady Margaret.'

Gerald Williams comments on the game of tennis, and Pam Shriver was inadvertently responsible for one of the very few clangers he ever dropped. Pam was stung by a wasp while she was playing at Wimbledon. She was in some discomfort, and she was looking down her dress to see if she could shake out the wasp. At that moment Gerald was talking about Pam and her tennis partner, and as she pulled her dress forward and looked down, he said, 'they are a fine pair, aren't they?'

I heard an Irish rugby football commentator – and it could only have been an Irish commentator – exclaim once during a game:

'Now one of the forwards has got the ball . . . I can't say who he is . . . yes I can . . . wait while I look at the programme . . . it's number eight . . . oh . . . well it doesn't really matter anyway, the other side has just scored a try.'

Neil Durden-Smith is an all-round sportsman, and commentates principally on hockey. On this occasion he was taking part in the Radio 2 *Sport Round-Up* programme, and

74

is credited with having the best excuse for missing a cue. The presenter of the programme handed over to Neil for his comments on a certain game, but couldn't raise him, so went on to the next item. Ten minutes later, he tried again, and found a very out of breath Neil, who gasped: 'I'm sorry. I can hardly speak. I have just run up the stairs to the box. I am late because I have been having tea with the Bishop of Leicester.'

Norman Cuddeford gives out the test scores and other cricket information on the *Today* programme. One day he thought that the presenter, John Timpson, was only rehearsing while another item went out live, so when John gave him his cue – 'So, Norman can you please bring us up to date with the score in the Test Match between England and Australia at Sydney?', Cuddeford larking around said, 'No, as a matter of fact I can't.' He then realised by Timpson's desperate signals that he was actually on the air. So, with the egg well and truly on his face, Cuddeford had to apologise, and then read out the scores.

Robert Hudson, when commenting on cricket, fiddles with things that are around him, pencils, papers, anything handy. Once he was fiddling with a rubber band attached to a score card, tweaking it up and letting it go. As he finished his commentary, he handed over to Freddie Brown, who was seated close by. At the very moment he did this, the rubber band slipped and shot across the box hitting Freddie very hard in the face. The result was that Freddie began his comments with a very loud yell of pain.

The Americans are deeply attached to their flag, which they revere, and their national anthem. They consider that they weld the nation together. Imagine the consternation that was caused during the Olympic Games in Los Angeles in 1984 when a BBC commentator, about to interview the British swimmer, Sarah Hardcastle, after she had won a silver medal, was heard to say, as the strains of the Star Spangled Banner rang out nearby, 'Oh, God, I can't do an interview against that racket.'

The 1984 Olympic Games were the occasion for some

unintentionally funny remarks by commentators. Here are some of them:

David Coleman on the 400 metres, 'He thinks it right to run the shortest distance, and he's absolutely right.'

Hamilton Bland commenting on the women's swimming, 'The girl who is not swimming will be in lane two, so there will be nobody in lane two.'

Brendan Foster commenting on Ovett, 'Ovett, he's not like Cruz, who is probably trying to impress people by winning.'

A commentator on the shot-putt, 'It's really like watching an eighteen-stone ballet dancer.'

A commentator about a gymnast on the high bar, 'She's really covering acres of ground.'

Ron Pickering on the gymnastics, 'There's no way she's given up on floor work. It's her best piece of apparatus.'

Hugh Porter on speed cycling, 'The riders are starting and finishing exactly where they are starting and finishing.'

Another commentator on cycling, 'You can see those wheels going round. The front wheel is rapidly followed by the back wheel.'

Harry Carpenter on one of the boxing bouts, 'If there is another round to go, anything could happen – but there isn't.'

It is sometimes quite difficult, when the pressure is on and the commentator is endeavouring to keep up the excitement, to avoid making remarks which when taken out of context like the above can sound ridiculous, even ludicrous. Personally, I think it all adds to the fun, and a commentator's ability to convey the excitement of the occasion is a most important part of his job. There were two lovely comments during swimming at the Olympics.

Alan Weeks, describing David Wilkie in action during one of the events, exclaimed, 'If Wilkie goes on like this he'll be home and dry . . .'

Peter Jones, in 1984, on one occasion greeted listeners with, 'Welcome to the Olympic Pool, where an enthusiastic crowd are cheering the exciting races which are taking place. I

have never seen such excitement. It's the pool that sets them alight.'

In the world of sport, all commentators realise that clangers and hiccups can easily occur. It is part of the hazards of doing 'live' television or radio; never knowing what is going to happen next.

Harry Carpenter who has been commentating on boxing for over twenty years told me of his most embarrassing moment, which was far worse than just a verbal slip-up. It was in the 1960s. He was commenting on a fight between the British Champion, Billy Walker, and an Italian, at Belle View, Manchester, which was being transmitted live. Billy managed to knock out the Italian in one and a half minutes flat. There was consternation in the control room where the producer, Ray Lakeland, was desperately wondering how to keep the show going, especially as the next bout was nowhere near ready to enter the ring. He quickly told Harry through his earpiece to get into the ring, interview Billy, and then go through the replay of the fight with him, which would be on the television monitor. Harry rushed down from his seat, climbed into the ring, and managed to talk to Billy. While he was talking he received a message through his earphone from the producer's assistant, saying, 'The tape's not ready, keep talking.' Harry being the true professional that he is then called in Billy Walker's brother, who was also Billy's manager, and talked to him for a while. He went on ad-libbing about the fight, waiting for a message over his earphone telling him the tape was ready for the replay. He was endeavouring with great skill to sustain the interest for the viewers, when suddenly a Steward of the British Boxing Board of Control, Joe Rashmon, shouted out, 'Get out of the ring, you're holding up the show.' Rather embarrassed, and feeling the egg was on his face, Harry scrambled out of the ring to do the commentary on the next fight. Unfortunately, worse was to follow. Back in his seat, Harry heard Ray on his earphone tell him, 'The tape is ready now, tell them that we'll show the replay before the next contest.' Harry immediately apologised to the viewers for the delay, and told them they were now going to see a replay of the whirlwind knock-out win by Billy Walker, and as he said to the viewers, 'Here it is...' a flyweight contest that had been on earlier came up on the screens.

Nick Owen, one of the presenters on TV/AM was originally a sports presenter and commentator. In his early days in radio he was reporting on a game that had taken place that day, when he received a message that there was an expert in the studio who could be brought in to give his comments. At an opportune moment this fellow was brought into the studio, and Nick introduced him – from the hastily passed piece of paper that he had received – and put his first question. Nick was horrified and embarrassed to discover that the man had a stutter. As a stutterer myself in my youth, I know that those who have this disability are not themselves embarrassed by it; it is usually those listening who become embarrassed for the person speaking with the impediment. On this occasion, Nick Owen was so concerned for the man, and his listening public, when the stutterer had difficulty with a word Nick endeavoured to help by finishing the sentence for him. Invariably it was the wrong sentence, which made this chap more determined to deliver the sentence he wanted to speak. This not only prolonged the interview beyond the allotted time, but created an embarrassing chaos as Nick endeavoured to bring the interview to a close, and the man with stuttering vehemence protested that he had not yet said anything on the subject that he had come to the microphone to talk about.

Sporting enthusiasts are a strange breed – and I should know, I am one myself! Here is a story in which a non-sportsman might have difficulty in understanding the attitude of the reporter quoted in it.

In May 1985, Alan Rusbridger, reviewing *The Weeklies* on Radio 4, told the listeners a sporting story which appeared in a magazine about a man who wanted to die on the tennis court. He was eighty years of age and it was his dearest wish to die in harness while playing tennis. He did just this, and everyone at his club was happy for him. The listeners were then told that the reporter of the story continued, 'He didn't go after serving an ace, but a double fault! I felt so sorry for him, it affected me more than the Bradford football disaster!'

6 · Royal Occasions

The broadcasting of Royal occasions, or any events in which royalty are involved must lend themselves more readily to clangers and hiccups than any other live show on radio or television. Not only is it impossible to rehearse for those big royal events that happen occasionally, such as a Jubilee, Coronation or Royal Wedding, but the technical side has to be planned on the basis that the presentation will be entirely impromptu. This presents a tremendous challenge to the production team, and when you think of an event like the recent wedding of Prince Charles to the then Lady Diana Spencer it is a tremendous tribute to the skill of everyone involved that they made such a marvellous presentation of this wonderful spectacle, a fact we tend to take for granted. In Britain we are used to this sort of event being handled with dignity and sensitivity by our television companies but when you are broadcasting to the world you can be forgiven a tiny error. One delightful slip-up came from Brian Johnston, who said at one point, '. . . I can see the bride's procession coming up Ludgate Hill. When she arrives below me here at St Paul's she will walk up the steps to the Pavilion . . . I mean the Cathedral.'

Such a minor slip on such a formal occasion is fun, though no doubt Brian felt a bit silly. An American broadcaster at the wedding of the Queen, then Princess Elizabeth, described the Yeoman of the Guard in their ceremonial dress for the folk back home thus: 'Near to me is one of these special King's police in his Tudor finery. These men are called Beefburgers, and each one holds a Halibut in his hand.'

Coronations as well as royal weddings present problems of organisation which must give many a headache to harassed officials. Following the crowning of George VI, radio listeners were amused to hear a voice picked up on a microphone that should have been switched off: 'What are we to do? The Barons are on the hoof and we haven't got the Earls away yet?'

Richard Dimbleby was one of the finest commentators on royal occasions. It was not only his style and delivery which was impeccable but also the content of his commentaries. The meticulous preparation that he put into every commentary made everything more interesting for the viewer or listener. There was an occasion in 1954 when the Queen Mother was due to visit the Royal School of Needlework. Richard was scheduled to give a commentary describing the exhibits before she arrived and then there was to be a fanfare and the Queen Mother would appear. He described everything within the allotted time, and then no trumpets ... and no Queen Mother. Having done his homework properly and having fully prepared himself, Richard started on another tour of the exhibition, giving a fluent account of the history of needlework in several countries. This lasted for a full twenty-five minutes, when to his relief he heard the trumpets. The Queen Mother appeared and walked straight up to him, and he was delighted to hear her say that she had been so fascinated by his commentary, which she had heard watching the television before starting out from Clarence House, that she had completely forgotten the time.

This wasn't the only time that Richard Dimbleby's thorough and conscientious preparation proved invaluable to him. Perhaps the most famous occasion was after the wedding of Princess Margaret. She was fifty minutes late starting out for her honeymoon and, with very little to talk about, Dimbleby kept the listeners interested with his continuous and fluent commentary. He showed such skill and professionalism that Anthony Craxton, the director, paid this tribute to him. 'The most remarkable aspect of this unexpected delay was that Richard wove his commentary into a masterpiece of continuity so that few people realised that what was being seen and said had not been planned in great detail beforehand. Unrelated subjects and objects were somehow, by Richard's description, made into a pattern at once seeming natural and flowing.'

It might be said that Richard Dimbleby's brilliance as a commentator was such that there was rarely, if ever, egg on his face. Situations that would leave other people covered with confusion, Richard Dimbleby carried off with style and panache. There was one classic occasion when the egg should have been well and truly in evidence, but being Dimbleby he carried off the whole embarrassing situation and no one listening ever realised that anything was wrong. It happened during the Queen's State Visit to Paris in the late 1950s when she was visiting the French Opera. Richard was seated deep down in the basement of the Opera House ready to do the commentary from a television monitor. Suddenly, without any warning his television monitor went dead; not only that, the lights failed and his telephone packed in as well. There was Richard, sitting in the dark, unable to contact his producer and his producer unable to get in touch with him. He knew that he was, in all probability, 'on air'. Calling on his imagination, and making use of his meticulous preparation, and at the same time listening to the sounds of the crowd outside, he managed to describe the scene. It was an incredible feat and one for which you would expect his employers to show great appreciation. When he arrived back in England, instead of being congratulated on his skill and expertise, he received complaints about his expenses, which were always, as he claimed, considerably less than a Fleet Street reporter of the same status.

Godfrey Talbot was the BBC's Court Correspondent at the time of the death of George VI in 1952. The King died at Sandringham during the night of Tuesday, 5 February. He was found dead by his valet in the morning. Even in the early 1950s BBC radio was not as organised as it is today, especially when it came to the news. Nowadays, a news item is included in a bulletin within a very short period of it happening, and something as important as the death of a King might well be put out as a news flash at the first available moment. Today specially prepared programmes would be on hand appropriate to the event. On this occasion the BBC was caught napping.

Godfrey Talbot was surprised on his arrival at Broadcasting House, on the morning of 6 February, to have Commander Colville, of the Palace Press Office, ring him and say curtly, 'Godfrey, when are you going to announce it on the air? What is going on?' Talbot was at a loss and replied cheerfully, 'Announce it? Announce what?' Colville told him that the King was dead, and that no announcement had been made by the BBC although it was already on the newstapes. Would Talbot please find out what was happening. In the newsroom Talbot found panic and confusion. The first news agency flash had been disbelieved, and when confirmation had come, nobody knew what to do. In those days programmes were never interrupted to give important information as they are today. News Officers were consulting rule books, confidential files and other BBC instructions, but nothing existed which stated how such an emergency should be dealt with. The usual light programmes were continuing, much to the annoyance of the Palace. Meanwhile, someone in authority was at last found to take a decision, and at 11.15 a.m. John Snagge sonorously gave out the news, 'It is with the greatest sorrow that we make the following announcement...' After the message had been read the BBC cancelled all its regular programmes. Listeners were left in a state of consternation. What was happening? Total silence from the BBC was unusual to say the least. The BBC decreed that nothing but solemn music should be played until the funeral on 15 February, nine days after the King's death. Even in Russia the death of the Head of State did not result in quite such a breakdown of normal broadcasting and, following the BBC's over-reaction to the King's death, a new set of rules were drawn to cover similar events in the future.

Once during a Royal Tour of India, Godfrey Talbot was having trouble with his tape-recording machine. He was squatting by the side of the road trying to change the tape, and a number of people kept coming up to him to talk. Talbot said, somewhat tersely, 'Do you mind, I can't talk now, the Queen will be here any minute, and I must have this machine ready.' He bent over the machine again, concentrating hard. He heard more people coming up to him and without looking up exclaimed, 'Please don't worry me just now, I must get this damned awkward tape threaded before they come.' He heard laughter, turned round, and there was the Queen and Prince Philip standing beside him.

Many years later Godfrey Talbot was covering another Royal occasion, the Prince of Wales' tour of the Principality after his investiture. By now the news bulletins were handled with much more style and professionalism, and interesting news was 'flashed in' whenever possible, as it occurred. The Prince's tour followed a hectic schedule, and this often meant that Talbot had to make use of any telephone which was handy to ring in his dispatches. There was no time to record them and then send them to the studio. By the time they arrived they would be dated. On one occasion Talbot, finding no public phone box available, dashed into a butcher's shop and rapidly explaining who he was asked if he could use their telephone. They kindly agreed, and when he got through to Broadcasting House he was asked if he would broadcast immediately, 'live', on *World at One* which was then being transmitted. The butcher's family had actually been listening to this programme and when Godfrey came over the airwaves, the butcher's wife, Mrs Jones, was absolutely incredulous. She said, 'Now I know they don't tell the truth. He can't be on the wireless as he's in our shop.'

Dorian Williams, that stylish commentator on all equestrian events, was always at his best when describing anything to do with Royalty – either taking part in horse shows, or describing them presenting prizes. He was caught out once when he thought his microphone was switched off and he was heard to exclaim about a Royal Lady, 'My God! What a hat!'

It can be slightly overwhelming for a commentator who doesn't normally cover royal occasions to find himself unexpectedly in the position of having to cover one. The Queen rarely visits cricket matches, but in 1969 she went to Lord's during the Test Match between England and New Zealand and the teams were presented to her. Robert Hudson, who was covering the match, inadvertently said, when the teams were being presented, 'It's obviously a great occasion for all the players. It is a moment they will always forget.'

These verbal slip-ups can occur so easily. John Snagge, at an Aldershot tattoo, introduced Queen Mary, as she arrived escorted by a military policeman on a motorbike, 'Here comes Queen Mary and her motorcycle.'

Probably the most embarrassing moment for John Snagge occurred during a commentary he made on the departure of the King and Queen to Canada in 1939. As their ship, HMS *Vanguard*, slipped out of the dock, with the bands playing and the crowd cheering, John described the scene magnificently and talked about the forthcoming tour. The tugs were having difficulty pulling the liner away from its mooring and the commentary went on longer than Snagge expected. He felt he was running out of material when a heaven-sent opportunity occurred. He saw the Queen say something to King George, and then she left the bridge on which she had been waving to the crowds. John explained to his radio listeners that the Queen had gone below. He then went on to describe something else that was happening, and then added, 'Ah. Now I can see water coming from the side of the ship.'

As I have said, BBC radio was not as highly organised back in the thirties as it is today. During the Coronation in 1937, the BBC set up a commentary box in front of Buckingham Palace in the charge of Neil Hutchinson. Nowadays no commentary box would be left unattended, or at any rate unlocked, especially if there was valuable equipment inside. In these dishonest days they would be lucky to find the box,

let alone the equipment, still there. On this occasion, after
Hutchinson had gone home one night, a young couple, finding the door of the commentary box open, went inside to
have a kiss and a cuddle. Later on, an engineer turned up,
and thinking the man inside the box was Hutchinson asked
him, 'Are you going to do the insert in the news?' The
young man, rather abashed at being found there stammered,
'Yes.' The engineer then handed him a microphone, and
told him to go ahead when the red light went on, and to
continue until it went off. The engineer then told the news
programme that all was ready. The young man suddenly
saw the red light go on, and somewhat nervously began to
describe what was happening outside the palace. He went
on talking until someone in control realised that it was not
Neil Hutchinson, and the item was quickly faded out. The
young man must have enjoyed telling his friends how he
described on the radio an historic occasion, just like Neil
Hutchinson.

When the Queen Mother launched the *Ark Royal* in the
1950s, Wynford Vaughan-Thomas was doing the commentary, but was told on no account to speak while the Queen
Mother broke the bottle of champagne over the bows of the
ship. He was to keep silent until the ship actually glided
into the water and then describe the scene. The Queen
Mother made her speech, broke the bottle, and the ship
moved off. She then turned and smiled in her gracious way,
and the producer, Ray Lakeland, seeing this on camera,
immediately 'punched it up' on the screen. Wynford following instructions started to describe the ship and the whole
scene, not knowing what was on the screen as he had no
television monitor there. The viewers were amazed to have
a picture of the Queen Mother accompanied by, There she
is, the huge vast bulk of her . . .'

And talking of being unintentionally rude Max Robertson
once introduced the Queen of Norway by saying she looked
very attractive in an 'off the hat face'.

Esther Rantzen was to do the commentary at the British
Academy of Film and Television Arts, where the awards

were to be presented by Princess Anne. As is customary nowadays on these occasions, Esther was wearing a radio microphone. This meant that the transmitter, which is about the size of a pack of cards, was fitted under her dress in the small of her back; the microphone being clipped to the front of her dress. This was done in preparation for her commentary, but first Esther stood in line to be presented to Her Royal Highness. The sound engineers discovered at the last minute that there was something wrong with her transmitter, and it was decided to change it. There was no time for Esther to retire so she just hoisted her dress above her head, while the sound assistant changed the transmitter. Unfortunately, the timing wasn't very good. As this was happening Princess Anne entered, and Roger Moore, who was the other compère for the evening, welcomed Princess Anne and then turned to introduce Esther; who at that precise moment was exposing her Marks & Spencers' down below and her face was covered by her dress. At least in that position no one was able to see the egg on her face!

One of the most tragic and dramatic broadcasts ever made was that of King Edward VIII on the occasion of his abdication. What is not so widely known is that the King wished to make a broadcast *before* this, stating his case to be allowed to marry Mrs Simpson so that the nation could know the facts and express its opinion. Confident that his Prince Charming image would over-ride any moral considerations, Edward VIII thought that if he made this broadcast the nation would be overwhelmingly in favour of his marriage. This would, of course, have been unconstitutional. A King cannot appeal over the head of his government to the people. As Mr Baldwin, then Prime Minister, said to him, 'What I want, Sir, is what you told me you wanted: to go with dignity, not dividing the country, and making things as smooth as possible for your successor. To broadcast would be to go over the heads of your Ministers and speak to the people. You will be telling millions throughout the world – among them a vast number of women – that you are determined to marry one who has a husband living.

They will want to know about her, and the press will ring with gossip, the very thing you want to avoid. You may, by speaking, divide opinion: but you will certainly harden it.'

On 10 December 1936, the Instrument of Abdication was signed and witnessed by the King's three brothers. The King was determined that on his abdication, being once more a subject, he could and would broadcast to the Nation. As a courtesy, he allowed Baldwin and the Cabinet to see his speech, on which he had worked hard and long.

How was the ex-King to be introduced on the air? This was what was exercising the minds of high-ups at Broadcasting House. Sir John Reith, the Director-General of the BBC, had decided that he, himself, should introduce the ex-King and had proposed calling him Mr Edward Windsor. The new King, George VI, said that it was impossible for him to become a plain Mr as he was born the son of a Royal Duke, and that at least made him a Lord. The new King commanded that the ex-King should be introduced as 'His Royal Highness Prince Edward'. Later he had the title of Duke of Windsor bestowed on him.

In the Augusta Tower the BBC had set up a studio and Sir John Reith was waiting. The Duke was asked to read a newspaper report about his brother's prowess at tennis for a voice test! Then, when the time for the broadcast approached Sir John Reith stepped forward and bent in front of the ex-King to announce into the microphone: 'This is Windsor Castle, His Royal Highness Prince Edward.' As he stepped backwards, Sir John knocked the microphone and this most historic speech was marred by a very audible 'clunk'.

7 · *Commercial Breaks*

Advertising came into broadcasting in this country for the first time in 1955. Previous to that the only advertising heard over the airwaves in Britain was from Radio Luxembourg. The debates in Parliament the previous year when the television bill was introduced, were heated and acrimonious. Many people sensed that a new, independent television channel funded by advertising revenue might well affect not just our viewing habits but our whole way of life. Those who argued most passionately against it, feared that commercial broadcasting would erode our traditional attitudes and values. As it has turned out, they were in many ways quite correct, though I am sure the introduction of commercial broadcasting in Britain was inevitable. Many major social changes that have occurred in our society during the last three decades owe something to the influence of commercial television. A lot of these changes have been for the better, and the standard of commercial television in this country has been extremely high. One of the immediate results of the creation of the independent television companies was a marked increase in the standard and professionalism of BBC television. The quality of the BBC's programmes had always been high, but they had become a little dull and complacent with no competition and nothing to stir them into being more adventurous. The BBC now had to recognise it needed to please what had previously been a captive audience.

The great blessing for everyone in this country was that the effects of sponsored television in America had been observed, and it was felt necessary to ensure that advertising only occurred in 'natural breaks', approximately every fifteen minutes of transmission time. This meant that the programme makers were protected from the worst excesses of commercialism, and were able to produce quality programmes which were not interrupted every few seconds by advertising, or 'A word from our sponsor', as happens in the United States. The ITA, the Independent Television Authority, was formed (with the introduction of commercial radio, it became the Independent Broadcasting Authority – the IBA) and became the controlling authority for commercial television in this country. They not only awarded the franchises for every television station, they laid down certain guide rules, about what could or could not be done in a programme. Unsolicited advertising that might creep into a programme accidently or on purpose was one concern of the ITA and there were rigid guide rules with regard to 'giveaway programmes'. There were to be only two shows giving major prizes to the public on the television network in any one week. There could be three in any one area. The top prize in any quiz or game show was to be limited to £1,000. That was in 1955 and the rules with regard to prize money only changed as recently as the late 1970s, in spite of the television companies regularly requesting an increase in the amount of the top prize.

The concession was only made, curiously enough, because of the programme in which I have been involved for many years, *Sale of the Century*. When this show first started in 1971 we always had a top prize in the final 'sale' of a motor car, and at that time there were about twenty small cars on the road which were under £1,000. Within six or seven years there were only three cars under £1,000 on the market and they were all foreign. The IBA refused to alter their rules and increase the figure for the top prize to over £1,000. The Press not being aware of these rules, criticised our programme for always offering foreign cars as the top prize, and some papers made a great issue of it. Anglia Television, who produced *Sale of the Century* had to explain tactfully the IBA ruling, and it was not long after that things were changed.

The motor car is a status symbol in the eyes of the public and is therefore an ideal major prize in a quiz, and the IBA recognise this. In the late 1970s they made the changes in keeping with the increased price of cars, and more recently as the price of a small British car has risen there have been further changes. Now a quiz show can offer an individual prize up to £1,750 and a major prize of £3,500 (this is to cover the price of a car) but not every week, and all this is conditional on the total money given away over a four-week period, not exceeding £17,500.

There had been an occasion a number of years previously when the ITA was acutely embarrassed by a quiz game. It was shortly after commercial television began in this country and the viewing public were experiencing their first taste of quiz shows, and the most glamorous one was an adaptation of an American programme, *The 64,000 Dollar Question*. In this country it was called *The 64,000 Question* and was compèred by Jerry Desmonde. The contestant going for the major prize answered a number of questions on the subject of his choice and if successful came back the following week to attempt more difficult questions for twice the amount of money, building up to the finale, in which the questions were very difficult, and the contestant if successful could win £1,000. That was a lot of money in 1956.

I remember the show well. The first contestant who was successful in winning this major prize was an actor. He had understudied me some years previously in a play, and as far as I knew had done little acting since that date. I was most impressed that he knew so much and I was amazed when he was successful in answering the very difficult questions to become the first person to win £1,000 on British television. I did not suspect, nor did anyone else, that there was anything unusual about his success. According to reports in the newspapers, to establish the show and increase its ratings the promoters had given the 'contestant' some of the answers secretly in advance of each show. The television company, ATV, who were transmitting the programme, and Jerry Desmonde were completely unaware of what was going on. When the truth came out some time later everyone concerned with the programme was extremely embarrassed, not least the ITA. As a result of this incident, the ITA created very strict ground rules for quiz games. The questions had to be prepared in secret and put into a sealed envelope not to be opened until the day of transmission – or nowadays on the day of recording. Even now, the IBA monitors quiz shows very carefully and occasionally sends their local representatives to 'sit-in' on a recording to be sure that everything is being fairly organised and carried out and their rules strictly adhered to.

When commercial television began, there were advertising magazine programmes – nicknamed 'ad-mags'. Each ran for approximately thirteen minutes. There was a setting and a story line, in which any number of different products was introduced and their qualities extolled by those presenting or taking part. The most famous, and probably the most successful 'ad-mag' was *Jim's Inn*, presented by Jimmy Hanley. The setting was a pub in which a number of regular characters appeared, and different products were discussed each week. A firm would buy so many minutes of time in the 'ad-mag' to have its product discussed and displayed. The advertiser supplied the script they wanted spoken, and that was then woven into an overall story. I was inadvertently responsible for bringing these particular programmes to a close. I had made some commercials for a travel firm called 'Blue Cars'. The following year I was contracted through my film production company to write and produce three more commercials for them and an 'ad-mag', as well as a conventional travel film. Blue Cars had a big following in the southern area, so they decided to buy the whole of the time on the 'ad-mag' which was being transmitted by Associated-Rediffusion. Whether Rediffusion thought that the travel company was going to promote other travel firms and travel products in this fifteen-minute slot, I don't know. Things were far more casual in those early days of commercial television, when everyone was struggling to get programmes made and on the air and the television companies were not as experienced and organised as they are today.

Blue Cars asked me to make a fifteen-minute programme promoting their holidays in different parts of Europe. I thought of an amusing way of doing this in which I was apparently having a party and showing some friends my holiday film when I am interrupted by the plumber. The plumber was Arthur Haynes who very kindly agreed to appear in the film for a modest fee as a guest celebrity talking with me about Blue Cars holidays. The programme was successful and the client was well pleased with the results. After its transmission, Rediffusion were embarrassed when the ITA pointed out that it was not permitted to promote only one product in an 'ad-mag' programme, since this was tantamount to sponsored television which was completely against the rules as laid down in independent television's charter. It was argued that there was nothing that stated that a television company could not devote the whole of an 'ad-mag' to one product since it was made quite clear to viewers that an 'ad-mag' was one long advertisement. The ITA decided that the rules that governed 'ad-mags' were too loosely formulated and they were very sensitive about having anything on the air which might be interpreted as sponsorship. So shortly after the transmission of this particular programme, 'ad-mags' were banished from television.

There was another 'ad-mag' which was withdrawn from television for quite a different reason. Bernard Breslaw, Clive Dunn, and Mario Fabrizi all appeared together in an 'ad-mag' programme for Harrison Gibson's store, and created a tremendous interest in that firm's products and no doubt increased their business. One customer, however, complained to the store that it was all wrong to see comedians appearing in a film promoting such a high quality establishment as theirs. Harrison Gibson took this complaint very much to heart and cancelled their contract with the company making the 'ad-mag'.

'Ad-mags' were always transmitted live and had their fair share of clangers and hiccups. In one programme there was a chunk of spam, which had been dressed with mayonnaise. The representative from the advertising agency, who was in the studio control room, decided that the spam was not in sufficient close-up and asked the director if the camera could move in closer. The director gave this instruction, and as the camera zoomed in on the spam, a blue-bottle alighted on the mayonnaise. In close-up, the fly on the screen looked like a monster from outer space.

In another 'ad-mag' the script required an actor to swallow a mouthful of beer and then say, 'It's delicious.' The actor didn't like the look of the beer so he only pretended to drink it during rehearsals. On the recording he managed to gulp it down, and then unfortunately pulled a rather sour face which infuriated the beer company. To pacify them, they were given a free spot in a later show.

There was a most unfortunate hiccup on another occasion. An ad-man who had been present at rehearsal was not happy about the way his client's products were being shown in the programme. He requested that they should be positioned differently but when the live transmission started the products were still not pointing the way that he wanted. In frustration he burst on to the set during the action shouting, 'I'll do it myself', which didn't help the programme or the continuity, let alone the actors taking part.

Margot Lovell, who used to be a presenter on one of Rediffusion's advertising magazines, dropped two clangers, which left her standing before the viewers with 'egg on the face'. This was at a time when all programmes went out live, so mistakes could not be rectified. When the script is advertising a product it is almost impossible to ad-lib your way out of a difficult situation. You always end up making matters worse. On this occasion Margot picked up a bottle of PLJ lemon juice and looking directly at the camera said, 'This bottle contains the juice of no less than twelve lovely oranges.' The other clanger which embarrassed her very much occurred when she was demonstrating the advantages of a dish-washing machine. She held up a cup which had been daubed with lipstick. Actually it was shoe black representing lipstick, since this was the era of black-and-white television and shoe black looked more effective on the screen. Margo told the viewers that she was going to demonstrate how the washing machine removed even lipstick stains. She put the cup with the lipstick mark into the machine, in which there were eleven other cups of the same kind. The machine was then switched on and she explained that the whole washing programme would run for about half an hour but as there was no time to go through the whole cycle she would switch it off and show the viewer what the cup would look like at the end of the wash. The machine came to a halt, and she put her hand inside to take out one of the clean cups to demonstrate the finished result. Unfortunately, she was unable to see which cup was the dirty one but realising the chances of her taking out that cup were eleven to one, she took out the first available one, proudly showed it to the viewers, stating, 'That's what your cup will look like when it's been through this washing process.' She then saw to her horror that she had taken out the cup that she had put in, and was actually showing the viewers the side with the lipstick still smeared on it. There was no explaining that one away!

The first television commercial was for Gibbs SR toothpaste, in which Margaret Smith appeared and the 'voice-over' was by Alex Mackintosh. Over-excitement, or first-night nerves, affected the technician in charge of punching up the programmes that were being transmitted on ITV's opening night and the button was pushed too soon on this commercial, with the result that the clock, the visual count-down in seconds, appeared on the screen before the commercial. In the early days of independent television the technique of interrupting a programme at the right moment, or finishing on time to bring in the commercials, had not been perfected. Sometimes programmes were faded before they were finished which could be very embarrass-ing. Debates or discussion programmes were occasionally clipped short in mid-sentence and a play, Thornton Wilder's *The Bridge of San Luis Rey*, had its ending cut completely, which produced a torrent of letters from those who wished to know how the play finished.

Cigarette advertising was permitted in the 1950s and some of the most glossy and expensive commercials prom-oted different brands of cigarettes. A lot of money was spent on these commercials and they were the forerunners of the sophisticated commercials that we see today. Sexual allu-sions were inherent in the theme or message of a number of these commercials, the most memorable perhaps being the one for Players, in which a young couple are seen romping together happily through an idyllic woodland setting, with appropriately romantic music. At the end a woman's voice says, 'and *afterwards* we smoked our Players'.

Most cigarette commercials were highly successful but one famous advertisement was so powerful it had quite the opposite effect to what was intended. The campaign was for Strand Cigarettes. It was extremely well made, well filmed and well thought out. A young man in a trenchcoat was seen strolling alone through London at night, smoking a cigarette. The whole atmosphere of the commercial evoked a man searching for something. He leant against a lamp-post, drew on his cigarette and the 'voice-over' intoned, 'You're never alone with a Strand.' The commercial was liked by the viewers and even won awards, and its haunting theme tune was popular enough to be issued on a disc but it failed to sell Strand Cigarettes. It seemed no one wanted to identify with that lonely, loveless young man.

All kinds of hiccups have occurred during the making of commercials, some of which have been quite embarrassing. There is the story of a model in a commercial for liver salts. It took some time for the director of the film to get 'the take' exactly as he wanted. The model who was promoting the salts didn't have the sense to *sip* from the glass each time but swallowed a mouthful. After the fifth 'take' she

protested that she really couldn't drink any more salts without dire results and rushed off to the loo.

Actually I had a similar experience in the early days of commercial television, when I was asked to appear in a commercial for Jaffa Cakes. I happen to like these particular biscuits very much and in the commercial I had to eat a whole biscuit. The care that the film people take to make sure everything is exactly as the advertisers would wish it often means there are many rehearsals, and sometimes a great number of 'takes'. By the time we had finished rehearsing I had gone off Jaffa cakes. By the time we had finished the tenth 'take' I actually began to dislike Jaffa cakes. By the time we had finished the filming and there was a 'take' which pleased everyone, I was just able to stagger home before all the Jaffa cakes came back the way they had gone down. I hasten to say that despite this I am still a keen eater of Jaffa cakes.

A great deal of money is spent on making commercials and a lot of time and talent is expended on them. Advertising executives and copywriters agonise over minute details of the script, and producers, directors, lighting men and sound recordists spend much time in the studio creating the perfect vehicle for promoting the product. Some of today's commercials are brilliant examples of creative work and are highly effective aids to selling. Now and again, however, all that money and talent seems a bit 'over the top'. A film unit went to the Outer Hebrides to make a commercial that included a grisly bear. It was expensive enough going so far to do the filming but problems really began when the star went missing. The star in this case was a bear called Hercules. He was fifty-four stone and extremely clever. It was reported that he could even water-ski. He earned huge sums of money for his owners, and was insured for over half a million. For twenty-two days he roamed free obviously unwilling to face fame and the film cameras. He successfully eluded thirty-three soldiers, two helicopters, nine policemen and the whole population of the Island of Benbecula and was eventually captured on the neighbouring island of

North Uist. Hercules like the man in the Strand advertisement, clearly rather enjoyed being alone and like other big stars gave his director a hard time before delivering a fine performance. It is not recorded whether the production company ever recovered its losses or, indeed, from the experience.

Working with animals can be difficult and demanding in the simplest of situations. My experience with dogs, for instance, made Hercules look like a much more desirable co-star. I had been asked to make a commercial for a dog food called Stamina. I remember the executive from the advertising agency asking me if I liked dogs. When I explained that I thought I could get along with most animals, she explained the storyline of the commercial. I appeared on a desert island, incongruously dressed in black jacket and pin-stripe trousers, and wearing a bowler-hat – clothes I often wore in the currently successful *Arthur Haynes Show*. I had to say in the script: 'Alone at last! Now I can tell you all about Stamina ...' As soon as I mentioned the word 'Stamina', innumerable dogs, of all shapes and sizes, were supposed to appear from every direction and leap all over me to try and get at the Stamina. One could see this was not going to be easy to film. When the day for the filming arrived, I travelled to a small studio in Bushey, where I met an animal trainer who had brought a large collection of dogs. I changed into my pin-stripe suit and spent some time getting to know them. The dog-handler assured the director, and everyone else concerned, that his dogs would respond to his commands and on the given word rush forward and leap all over me in an apparent effort to get at the Stamina. We tried a rehearsal. The dogs seemed more interested in exploring the studio than leaping at me. We tried more rehearsals, with the dog-handler exhorting his animals to 'attack' and 'go fetch him boy'. The director then pointed out that as they wished to record only the dialogue that I was speaking together with the noise the dogs were making, it would be impossible to do this with the dog-handler's voice on the soundtrack as well. It was then decided that I should have some food smeared over my hand, which would attract the dogs to come and lick it.

Before we did the next rehearsal the dogs were introduced to the food that was going to be used – which incidentally was not the same food as in the tin – and on 'action' it was hoped that having been given the scent of the food they would all leap forward to try and acquire a little more of the mushy stuff that was oozing out between my fingers. Two or three of the more intelligent dogs got the hang of what was required but the remainder still went sniffing round the studio trying to discover where the food was. After many more rehearsals and attempts at some 'takes' which were not much more successful and which had taken up most of the day, it was decided to abandon the filming and try again on the following day.

When I arrived at the studio the next morning, and put on my city suit, which now smelt of stale dog food, I was told that a different group of dogs had been engaged, and I was introduced to their handler. He made me feel very confident right away by saying, 'Don't worry, Nick, I've been starving them since last night. They'll be ready to have a go as soon as they get the word.' We had learnt something from our experiences the previous day, so now more dog food was smeared over the jacket of my suit, along the arm and round my hand and underneath the tin of Stamina. The director decided to try a 'take' right away in the hope that, with the dogs fresh, it might all happen right away. It was not much better than the previous day. The dogs were affected by the atmosphere and the lights, and while most of them could smell food, they were puzzled as to where to find it. More dog food was smeared over my black jacket, which was now becoming quite saturated, and rather evil smelling! We tried further 'takes'. Some of the cleverer dogs were now getting to know their part and jumped up to lick my clothes. I decided that the best way to act the scene was to pretend to fall over when the dogs jumped up at me, so they could crawl all over me and appear to be licking the tin of Stamina in excitement. I would then shoot up from the midst of this canine melée to proclaim the virtues of this dog food.

One of the stage crew then said that dogs went mad for aniseed, so somebody went in search of this dog-provoking substance while we broke for lunch (not that I was very hungry, and no one wanted to sit next to me). After lunch, I climbed back into my jacket, which was now becoming as stiff as cardboard with the dried-up dog food, and the aniseed was added to the very pungent smells that were issuing from the ruined material but being black it fortunately still looked quite presentable.

We tried another 'take'. More dogs got the idea of what was required. This encouraged the dog-handler and the director to smear more aniseed on me, and really cover me from top to toe with dog food. It was pushed down my collar, behind my ears, around the rim of the bowler, on my trousers, in the pockets of my jacket; some was even put under the rim of my bowler so that it got into my hair, in the hope that when my hat fell off the dogs would lick my head. In this unbelievable revolting state we began the next 'take'. By this time, some of the dogs went for me on cue but others less bright still could not understand that I was 'food'. They barked loudly but refused to leap at me.

The director was by now desperate. More food and aniseed, and this time also some bacon fat, was smeared over me and lumps of meat and bacon lodged wherever it could be concealed. We went for another 'take', and this is the one I will always remember. I stepped into camera shot, and spoke the opening line, 'Alone at last! Now I can tell you all about Stamina ...' The dogs were released, more than before came bounding towards me, I fell to the ground as if knocked over by the rush, and all seemed to be going well. I was trying to tell the viewers about the quality of Stamina, while covered with frantic canines of all descriptions licking every part of my prostrate figure. Unfortunately, two of the animals, who had not yet had a lick, picked up the attractive scent for the first time, and barking furiously leapt forward to have a taste, but they had picked up the scent from my lower regions on which they landed together with great force. There began a dog fight for the meat that was clinging to my trousers which seemed to endanger my life and limbs. I leapt up to my feet before these two ferocious animals could cause me irreparable physical damage and ruin my married life into the bargain! The director, in the tradition of show business, asked aggressively, 'What was wrong? Why did you run away. It was going so well.' When I explained what had happened he was more sympathetic, but asked if I would do it again as quick as possible while the dogs were in the right mood. I said I wasn't very happy about the mood of one or two of the dogs, and I asked if anyone had a cricket box that I could wear. Since this could not be found at short notice, and it appeared the dogs were straining at the leash to get back at the evil smelling food-encrusted suit, I compromised by putting on two jockstraps so at least my most vulnerable areas were protected in the event of a dog fight starting up again.

Now feeling rather nervous, we went for another 'take'. It seemed that this might be the one to go 'in the can'. I certainly hoped so. Even more food and aniseed were smeared over me, and for good luck they also put some chocolate in with the food, so once the dogs discovered the source of supply, they would continue to enjoy themselves. With my hand barely able to hold the tin of Stamina for all the gooey dogmeat in my palm, and smelling like something that had stepped out of an old dustbin, I felt I never wanted to open a tin of dog food again. Gritting my teeth, and trying at the same time to present a happy relaxed personality to the camera, I stepped forward on the word, 'Action'.

On cue, the dogs were released, the barking seemed to be more intense than before, and praying that this was the 'take' that would work, my professionalism overcame my anxieties, and I threw myself into the action. With dogs leaping all over me, I pretended to fall to the ground, and as these excited creatures started licking me, my bowler was knocked adrift and one dog found the food in my hair. I got

out the lines extolling the qualities of Stamina, and rose to my knees with the dogs still barking excitedly round me to deliver the pay-off line. The job was finished, I really felt I had earned my money that day. If only it had been just *egg* on my face.

In the early days of broadcasting when there was only the 'wireless', the BBC was most meticulous in making sure that no product of any kind was ever mentioned in a broadcast. I remember this being a problem when we started the first radio satire show, *Listen to this Space*, which was a breakthrough in radio at the time. When we began the first series, it was found necessary to quote from various newspapers. Up to that date the mention of a newspaper was held to be advertising. We managed to obtain permission to say the names of the papers on the understanding that throughout the series nearly every paper would be mentioned at some time or other so we would not be mentioning one at the expense of the others. It is interesting to note that as a result of the BBC giving permission to our show to mention the names of newspapers, it became common practice and now no one thinks anything about it. One can imagine how inhibiting were the rules concerned with advertising in the very early days of broadcasting.

The former Essex cricketer, Canon F. H. Gillingham, was once giving a commentary on a cricket match being played at Leighton between Essex and the New Zealand touring team. His first broadcast on this match coincided, unfortunately, with a twenty-minute interval, and in those days there was no team of commentators who could discuss progress and comment on the day's play. There were no statisticians to help out with facts and figures that might interest the listener. The Canon spent ten of the twenty minutes telling listeners what had happened in the match so far. Finally, realising he had nothing further he could say, he began, in desperation, to read out the advertisements on the hoardings around the ground. The senior executives at the BBC who heard this were horrified, but in those days there was no means of communicating with a commentator 'on air'. Poor Gillingham was, however, well and truly made aware of his error when his stint of commentating ended.

Other countries have equally strict codes of practice with regard to advertising in broadcasting, and sometimes it seems a little weird the way they interpret them. In Australia an enterprising mineral water company hired a girl who looked like Lady Diana Spencer, as she was then, to advertise their product, wearing a copy of the famous low-cut black dress in which Lady Diana had caused such a sensation. The Australian Television Authorities, however, insisted that it should be made quite clear that the girl was a model and not the fiancée of the Prince of Wales, so the commercial carried a warning, which read: 'Beware! This is not the real Lady Di. Do not be misled!'

8 · *Drama Shows*

Drama shows nowadays are all recorded in advance. Most of them in this country are shot in the television studio and recorded onto video tape, a scene at a time, and edited together later. Any outside film sequences are transferred on to the master tape at the final editing. A similar procedure is followed in radio except that it is quicker, since no memorising of words or movement is involved. The producer can often 'rehearse record' the play scene by scene. The programme is assembled and edited to time later. If any clangers or hiccups occur, the scene is immediately reshot or re-recorded, so most of the stories about things going wrong in plays date from the years *before* recording took the excitement out of broadcasting.

In the early days of *Z-Cars*, that highly successful police series, which was the model for many others and which featured a number of actors who are now stars, a situation arose which would be impossible today. On live television most of the show was transmitted from the studio and there were a few outside sequences on real roads, pre-filmed, to which the director cut on cue as the programme was going out. In one episode Joe Brady and Brian Blessed, playing police constables, were to be shown driving up to the police station. Then the scene was cut to reveal James Ellis as P.C. Lynch at the station desk, speaking into a telephone. He was to put the telephone down, make an entry in the day-book and then look up as the other two entered.

The car could not be driven in the studio so it was dragged in by the stage crew. The programme began, transmitted 'live' don't forget, and the car appeared to drive up to the police station. It came to a halt but the car door wouldn't open to let the driver get out. Because of the way it had been positioned, there was not enough room to get out of the car on the passenger side so both 'policemen' were stuck in the car. The director guessed what must be wrong and quickly cut his cameras to James Ellis, as P.C. Lynch, who was waiting for his cue. Jimmy spoke his lines into the phone, put it down, and then started to write in the day-book as rehearsed. Suddenly the phone rang – this was not in the script – but in a live show one has to be ready for anything. Jimmy, keeping in character, picked up the phone; it was the director, and his voice sounded desperate, 'Jimmy, we've a problem; keep acting; but listen, the car's stuck: ad-lib until we can release the others then they will walk in.' Jimmy, a real professional, muttered something appropriate into the phone, and then put it down. He continued muttering something about entering the information in the day-book. It is reported that he then said, 'Oh dear, oh dear,' several times in character, which must have come from the heart! Then he heard a noise, looked up and saw, to his relief, Joe Brady and Brian Blessed walk into the station. Sustaining the scene, Jimmy said aggressively, and rather pointedly, 'What kept you?' 'We were stuck in the car,' replied Joe nonchalantly, and they then continued with the scene as scripted. No one watching at home was aware how close things had been to disaster.

Another embarrassing situation occurred during a transmission of *Z-Cars*. It concerned the young Prince of Wales, who was visiting the studios to see how the show was put together. He was talking with Jeremy Kemp and another actor on the set, while the preliminaries to shooting the show were being gone through. The floor manager – or studio manager as they are now called – is an autocrat on the set, and in complete charge of what takes place in the studio. He is linked by radio microphone to the producer or director in the control room. On this occasion he asked for silence. Prince Charles, not realising that it applied to him, went on chatting. The floor manager then called, 'Shut up over there, silence!' One voice carried on, much to the floor manager's fury. He bellowed, 'WHEN I ASK FOR BLOODY SILENCE, I MEAN BLOODY SILENCE!' The twelve-year-old young Prince stopped in mid-sentence and blushed as red as a beetroot. Fortunately, the floor manager never knew what he had done, or I am sure he would have blushed a deeper red! For once 'egg' was on a Royal face!

In the early days of play production when everything was going out live, the play was rehearsed and then performed much as it is in the theatre, with the exception that the actors had to remember to which set they had to move. It helped if the actor could be aware of which camera was operating, so he didn't cross another actor's shot. Each camera has a red light on top, which goes on when that camera is transmitting. In those days each studio had three cameras. Brian Forbes once had a nerve-racking experience. In a particularly difficult part he turned, as rehearsed, for camera 1 to take the shot, and to his horror he saw out of the corner of his eye that it was surrounded by technicians who were taking it to pieces. The floor manager signalled to Brian that he should turn to favour camera 2. This meant adjusting the rehearsed moves for fear of 'masking' the other actors. As he turned and altered his prepared position, the red light on camera 2 flickered, went out and started emitting large quantities of smoke. The director ordered camera 3, through the headphones, to try and find a position to shoot the scene. The floor manager desperately tried to indicate to Brian that camera 3 was going to transmit what was left of the scene. Brian gamely struggled on and finished his speech as if nothing was wrong. Once again chaos and disaster had been held at bay by a whisker!

Alaistair Scott Johnson was for many years a producer in radio 'light entertainment'. He was a most experienced man of radio, having worked for the BBC most of his life. He started as a sound-effects boy in 1939, and one of the prestigious programmes on which he worked in that capacity was a play about the origins of the 1914–18 war. The programme was, of course, going out live, and Alaistair was handling six turntables on which the effects were played. He had 'shot' the Archduke Ferdinand right on time, but then one table caught on fire. The only option left open to him in a live show was to ignore it, and carry on with the other five turntables, while trying to put out the fire as best he could. There was no one else to help him, and he was several floors away from the studio where the actors were performing. The producer started to harass him through the 'talk-back', but Alaistair was too busy to give a coherent reply as he was trying to cope with all the sound cues on five turntables when he needed six, and at the same time extinguish the fire. Fortunately, someone who happened to pass by, noticed smoke coming from the studio, looked in, saw what was happening, hurried to the nearest fire extinguisher, came back and squirted it at the flames. The situation, as well as the show, was saved, and there was no 'egg' on Alaistair's face, just a little fire-extinguisher foam!

Desert Island Discs is in the *Guiness Book of Records* as the longest running radio show. Roy Plomley, who created this programme, must have interviewed more people than anyone else in radio. The programme covers a very broad spectrum of people from all walks of life, who are invited to be cast away on Roy's mythical desert island. He had long wanted to interview the thriller writer, Alistair Mac-Lean, but MacLean was a very busy man who rarely gave interviews. He asked his staff to discover if MacLean could be persuaded to be a castaway. To Roy's delight, within a few days he was told that MacLean had agreed. After telephoning the number given him and explaining how the show was recorded, Roy invited MacLean to have lunch with him at the Savile Club on the day of the broadcast, which was his usual procedure. Roy had read all the relevant press-cuttings, read MacLean's latest novel and thoroughly briefed himself. He arrived at the club and was quite surprised when someone who didn't look very much like MacLean in his photographs appeared. Roy reflected that people sometimes do look different in photographs. The man had a cheerful, warm personality and Roy thought that the programme was going to be a success. He was, however, slightly puzzled that the man mentioned several recent visits to Canada, but he decided that MacLean had probably been there on promotional trips concerned with his writing. Being such a busy man, Roy asked, 'Which part of the year do you put aside for writing books?' 'I am not Alistair MacLean the writer,' the man replied. Roy looked dumbfounded. 'I'm in charge of the European Tourist Bureau of the Government of Ontario.'

Roy realised there was no turning back. He must not embarrass the man, and at the same time he had to discover something relevant for the show. The two men went upstairs to lunch, and discreetly Roy asked questions in order to obtain information for an interesting interview in the show. He rapidly made notes as they ate, then they took a taxi to Broadcasting House where the two men went through the interview, and Alistair proved to be an ideal broadcaster, relaxed and humorous. Roy's producer was getting more and more puzzled, so he stopped recording, and called Roy out of the studio to ask when the interview would be getting on to MacLean's books. Roy explained the situation and the two men agreed it would be too embarrassing to send MacLean home, so they finished recording the interview. It was never broadcast, as they thought that MacLean of Ontario was not of general interest to the public, but he did receive a fee and an explanation that owing to a misunderstanding the programme would not be used.

Desert Island Discs has occasioned at least one motorcar accident. Charles Murland, a Governor of the Royal Ballet School, was listening in his car to ballerina, Nadia Nerina, give her choice of records, and heard her say, 'They did say at one time that I was the greatest technician in the West.' At that point Murland's car hit the one in front of him. Getting out he confronted the exceedingly angry driver of the other car. Murland apologised, explaining that he was listening to Nadia Nerina on *Desert Island Discs*. The other driver confessed he too had been listening to the programme and that Nerina's statement had caused him to brake hard to avoid a pedestrian. The two men looked at each other, and then shook hands.

The Man Born to be King was written by Dorothy L. Sayers, and was one of the greatest successes of radio broadcasting, but it very nearly didn't get off the ground and on to the air.

The time was the 1940s, and in those days there was still an embargo on representing God or Jesus Christ on the stage. The BBC was not, however, affected by this ruling, and so thought that a series of plays on the life of Jesus would be a splendid project. Immediately, of course, they ran into a lot of criticism from clergy and ordinary members of the public. The Lord's Day Observance Society were outraged by the idea, and issued a protest in the form of an advertisement in the Church of England newspaper. A question was even asked in the House of Commons and a meeting of the Central Religious Advisory Committee was called. The members of this committee read copies of the script of the first play in the series and were satisfied and voted thirteen to one to let the broadcast go ahead. The Governors of the BBC, however, were still not certain whether to proceed with the production. It seems that they were rather alarmed at all the controversy. Nevertheless, the series finally got the go-ahead.

The actual production was not without its difficulties. Originally, the plays had been intended for *Children's Hour*. Dorothy Sayers was not very pleased to hear that her favourite producer, Val Gielgud, would not be able to produce them. They would, however, be in the capable hands of 'Uncle Mac' – Donald McCulloch – the popular producer and presenter of children's programmes. Dorothy Sayers subjected him to a six-page memo on how to produce the.series. This didn't go down very well, and then there was more trouble when Miss Sayers submitted the first script. She was outraged to receive a letter from McCulloch's lady assistant outlining alterations that were wanted. Miss Sayers tore her script into many pieces and returned it to the BBC. The BBC, recognising that disaster threatened, hurriedly gave way and called in Val Gielgud to direct the plays after all. *The Man Born to be King* was a huge success. Everything about it was impeccable, the writing, the casting, the performances and the production.

In contrast to *The Man Born to be King*, another great BBC radio success was the thriller series, *Dick Barton*. This show ran for many years in the 1940s and 1950s, and the characters became household names. The success of the show was due in no small part to the producer of the series, Neil Tuson. The show was recorded but in those days this was not done very far in advance, and Neil told me of a situation that very nearly left him with egg on his face. The programmes were recorded in the old Grafton Theatre in Tottenham Court Road, one of the many delightful theatre studios in London that the BBC possessed in those days, and which now, for financial reasons, have disappeared. Except for audience shows, which come from the Paris studio in the West End, all other radio productions are from the more impersonal, but technically highly efficient, studios at Broadcasting House. At the Grafton there was a narrow corridor outside the studio with a microphone at one end and a loudspeaker at the other. This was used to give an echo effect – how times have changed! On this occasion, Neil needed a scream from an actress at a particular moment on page seven of the script that was being recorded. The actress went into the corridor, and the heavy door into the studio was shut. Neil was going to give her a cue light when to scream. The rehearsal began, and in the middle of page four he heard the most heart-rendering scream imaginable. He immediately pressed the talk back, and said, 'No, darling. It was magnificent, but not yet. It's on page seven. I'll give you the cue.' There was another scream, and a frantic and terrified voice came over the microphone, 'There's a rat in here. A rat. Let me out of here.' They rushed from the studio to help the petrified

girl. The rat shot through the studio creating more chaos, and it was some time before the poor girl could be calmed down. The scream that the girl gave on page seven was nowhere near as realistic as the one that she had uttered on page four!

The Archers is the longest-running radio serial and maintains a very high standard. To achieve authenticity, recordings of background sound and other effects are sometimes made in the actual situations where they occur, rather than being simulated in the studio. When meetings of the Women's Institute are held, the proceedings begin with the singing of *Jerusalem*. To make sure that they had the authentic sound for a scene that had been written to take place in the W.I. at Ambridge, the village around which the stories in *The Archers* revolve, the writer and creator of the series, Godfrey Baseley, arranged to have his own wife's W.I. recorded. The members there sang their hearts out for the recording. The piano had one or two notes that stuck, but that all added to the authenticity – or so Basely thought. After that particular episode of *The Archers* was transmitted, dozens of letters were received from all over the country, declaring that no W.I. would sing as badly as that, and the scene was a disgrace.

The Archers has a big following in the farming community, and the producers recognise that it is a vehicle for providing up-to-date information about farming methods. The writers, therefore, are very careful to see that the programme is not only authentic but up to date. When the serial first started, Dan Archer was the proud owner of a herd of Shorthorn cows. Several years later the writers noticed the Friesian cows were gaining in popularity, and decided that Dan should change his herd. This caused consternation with the Shorthorn society, who were anxious to protect the breed and the living of those members of the society who bred this kind of cattle. The changeover was delayed and an outbreak of foot and mouth disease had to be organised on Dan's farm to enable him to change over to producing beef. Much later this herd was dispersed and

Dan decided to take up milk production again – this time buying the now more popular Friesian cattle.

Central Television's *Crossroads* always keeps up a high standard of authenticity. In doing so, of course, it must not offend any existing organisation. So the firms, shops and businesses that are used by the motel all have fictional names. In its early days there was a storyline which involved a somewhat dishonest driving school. The scriptwriters wanted a name that was unlikely, memorable and effective so they chose the Pass Quick School of Motoring. Within a few minutes of the imaginary school being mentioned on the air there was a telephone call protesting. There really was a Pass Quick School of Motoring in Wolverhampton! Luckily the owner and his wife were *Crossroads* fans, and didn't take the matter any further.

There have been a number of occasions in *Crossroads* when the professionalism of the artists has saved the day. Noele Gordon was acting in a scene with her son, Sandy, played by Roger Tonge when he noticed that flames were coming out of an electric toaster. He drew Noele's attention to this. She turned round and saw the fire and, being the true professional that she is, calmly said, 'Put it out, Sandy' – which Roger did.

On another occasion, Margaret Lake accidentally put a tea towel on a stove. It immediately flared up, but she and Roger Tonge *ad libbed* while they put the fire out, making a very realistic scene for the viewers.

Roger Tonge was a victim of a bad motor accident, long before he became one as the fictional Sandy. In the real-life accident, Roger's right eyelid was severed and he had to have eighty stitches in his face! He also had two black eyes. The producer, Reg Watson, was very worried when he visited Roger because Roger had a very important scene to act within the next week. Roger said he felt that he could not work looking as he did but Reg insisted that he was fine and should be in the studio on the day required.

Roger turned up in a wheelchair, looking simply awful. The cast were worried but pretended not to notice Roger's appearance, until Noele Gordon pointed out that they could not just ignore it without looking foolish. Reg agreed, so extra lines of dialogue were written in to explain Roger's face. He was supposed to have walked accidentally through a plate glass window. As he had no time to learn his lines, some were pasted on to a newspaper, others into a book which he picked up and used as a 'prop'. The cast picked up the cues and everything was fine. Only one person was affected: the First Aid nurse at the studio. When she saw Roger she fainted.

The producer was much kinder to John Bentley when he had influenza. John, who played Hugh Mortimer, had a very important scene in an episode of *Crossroads* to be transmitted that week. It was decided that he was too ill to come to the studio, so a camera unit visited John at his sick-bed and filmed him in close-up speaking some of his lines. When the show was recorded later, another actor was seen from the back view for the reverse shots, with John's voice recorded over. The close-up shots taken at his bedside were edited in later.

The Independent Television Companies are governed by very strict rules and one rule, naturally, is that no product must be mentioned by name in a programme, otherwise the television company can be in breach of its contract. Also, other firms have paid large sums to advertise their products in the commercial breaks. In *Coronation Street*, all the food in the shop is 'own brand'. One firm, however, got round this ban when they were asked to supply a piece of machinery for a factory scene. The firm offered to do this free, provided they were allowed to photograph the set and use the picture for publicity purposes, but their offer was refused and a normal fee was paid. The firm, however, photographed the machine on its own and issued a leaflet of it with the caption, 'Watch *Coronation Street* at 7.30 p.m. on Monday next and see our new product in action.' Granada was left with egg on its face, determined not to be so bamboozled again – and the services of that firm were never requested again.

The producers of a popular television series have to be extremely careful to get every minute detail about a character right. The tastes, interests and idiosyncracies of each regular character have to be filed and referred to if they are to avoid letters of correction from ardent followers of the programme. In a very early episode of *Coronation Street*, Ena Sharples, played by Violet Carson, was heard to say that she didn't like chocolate éclairs. *Eight* years later she was seen, in an episode, eating not only one, but two éclairs. Dozens of letters pointing out the error confirmed how long and accurate are the memories of the fans of a show.

One of the greatest television drama undertakings was Granada Television's *The Jewel in the Crown*. Four months of the filming took place in India, and cast and crew underwent some colourful and uncomfortable experiences. It is the custom in India for a Sannyasi, or Holy Man, to bless the film being made on its first day, before any work has started. So in January 1982 a Holy Man turned up in Udaipur, where everyone was assembled for the first day's shooting. With the Sannyasi and his assistant was a little shrine. Four members of the unit were chosen to take part in the ceremony, barefooted. They were annointed and asked to pelt the shrine, and the Sannyasi, with flowers. The Holy Man then picked up a coconut and seemed about to throw it at the camera. The producer/director, Christopher Morahan, not wanting a valuable piece of equipment damaged, rushed forward and snatched the coconut from the startled Sannyasi. He then tapped the camera with it and filming began. Honour was satisfied and one small delay was avoided though India has many another up its sleeve!

Beggars were needed for one scene in *The Jewel in the Crown*, and it was decided to ask actual beggars to come along and be actors for the day. A group was found and persuaded to appear; they would be collected by coach and given a card which, at the end of the day, they would exchange for about thirty rupees. The first problem was that when the coach arrived the driver refused to have the beggars in it and he had to be persuaded, which took time.

Then the beggars refused to go! It turned out that they had been told that it was all a ruse to get them to hospital where they would be made to have a vasectomy. At last they were reassured. Then during the filming they protested vociferously. They couldn't understand why the actors weren't putting real money into their hands as they sat there 'begging'.

Eric Porter, playing Count Bronowsky, had to look older than he is in real life so his hair was bleached silver before he left for India. In Delhi he decided to have a swim in the pool of his hotel, and was dismayed when he came out of the water to find that the chlorine had acted on the bleach and turned his hair green! It was quite a challenge for the make-up department to get his hair back to the required colour.

Mysore racecourse boasts some of the finest turf in India, and had been hired for one scene by the film unit for this reason. A week before this scene was to be shot, the unit discovered to its horror that the turf had been set on fire to encourage its growth – apparently this was done regularly. To get it back to its beautiful green, the film unit had to water the course for a whole week, twenty-four hours each day. The expense of doing this was one thing, but the cost in lost filming time and altered schedules was even higher.

Long before the film unit arrived in India problems had arisen. The customs in India had been difficult. When filming abroad, it is necessary not only to obtain permission from the authorities concerned and negotiate with the local unions, but a detailed list of every single item of equipment and goods taken into that country has to be submitted to the customs officer. This is put on a *carnet*, and runs to many pages, with the serial numbers of each individual piece of equipment listed for checking at customs. Then a sum of money is placed with the appropriate authorities, which is released only when these technical goods are cleared out of the country by the customs who checked them in. Each country has different customs' regulations, with regard to both technical and non-technical goods. In

India everything has to leave the country after filming, except consumable goods. Granada had allowed *three weeks* for customs clearance which they thought would be more than enough since the forms had been meticulously filled in. The items, enough to fill nine lorries in three hundred containers, were documented under consumable and non-consumable goods. The Indian Customs decided that the contents of three containers had been put on consumable forms when they should have been put on non-consumable forms. All the three hundred packing cases would have to be flown back to Manchester, from where they came, and the forms altered and the crates returned to India again! This would have cost a small fortune – when lost filming was taken into account. There was panic at the studios back in England. Phone calls across continents, delicate negotiations with important officials, in both countries, eventually produced – at the last moment – a solution. Granada agreed to pay an even higher refundable indemnity to have the goods accepted on the existing forms.

When the final scenes of *The Jewel in the Crown* were to be shot, an old station in Buckinghamshire was used, and the local Job Centres found over a hundred Indian people to act as extras. The scene was a gruesome one – a mob attacks a train leaving many dead and wounded behind. The filming was held up – which costs money, especially when a large crowd is involved – because one man refused to play as requested. He had been on a pilgrimage to Mecca, and he felt this made it beneath his dignity to pretend to be dead.

9 · Comedy Shows

We expect funny things to happen in comedy shows – it wouldn't be a very good comedy if they didn't. Things, however, can still go wrong in the world of comedy. It is just that it is less embarrassing than when it occurs in other fields of entertainment, since the people involved in comedy are playing for laughs. Obviously the more serious and solemn the occasion or event, the more acutely the actor or presenter feels the situation, and the funnier it becomes to the observer. A comedian thrives on spontaneity, and a good comic is usually a very good *ad-libber*, so if something goes wrong in a comedy show the instinct is to capitalise on the situation, and turn it to one's advantage. If an audience is aware of what has gone wrong, they invariably enjoy the show much more and laugh louder, and every audience admires a clever *ad-lib*, especially in a difficult situation.

Disasters can always occur in programmes that go out live. *The Arthur Haynes Show*, in which I appeared as the straight man to that wonderful comedian, was transmitted live for a number of years in the late 1950s and early 1960s. There is something special about a live show. What it lacks in polish, it invariably makes up for in spontaneity. If something does go wrong, then one's adrenalin pumps away more and more vigorously to help one cope with the situation and cover any embarrassment.

Many marvellous sketches were written by Johnnie Speight for Arthur Haynes and myself to perform over the years, and many tricky situations occurred, but two stand out in my mind. The first was a sketch in which I played a well-heeled young man in an expensive flat, sitting down to enjoy a quiet evening with a book, when I hear the distant sound of a fire engine bell. The whole point of the sketch was that Arthur Haynes, as a fireman, bursts into the room with his crew, and in spite of my remonstrations and angry insistence that there is no fire in my flat, proceeds to behave as if the fire is there and I am suffering from what he calls 'fire-panic'. When I complain that the water is ruining my precious antiques, he orders his crew to salvage them, and so the sketch proceeds until I am left soaked to the skin and the flat is ruined. In the end the firemen discover they have come to the wrong address – of course! The problem with this sketch was that we could never rehearse with the fire hose because the water would ruin the furniture and set and this could not be rebuilt in time for the show. We rehearsed the dialogue and movements, and mimed the action with the hose. I remember that the resident fireman did take me out behind the Hackney Empire – from where the show was transmitted – and covered me in oilskins and then turned the hose on me to demonstrate its power. Even at half-cock it had a tremendous force, so at least I was ready for this.

To do a comedy show 'live' is a challenge under the best of conditions; to do it when you are unable fully to rehearse with the 'props' is even more dangerous. For this sketch they had put down a tarpaulin to cover the floor, since there was bound to be a fair amount of water, but everyone had overlooked how long the sketch was going to run and just how much water would accumulate. It all started very smoothly, until the moment when Arthur Haynes as the leading fireman smashed down the door with his axe and burst into the room, closely followed by two other firemen with a hose ejecting gallons of water in a powerful spray which completely knocked me off my feet. I picked myself up, but the firemen continued to spray me rather than the room where the fire was supposed to be raging. The audience in the TV theatre loved this – and so did the technicians, since it was totally unexpected. Worse was to follow. The tarpaulin on which we were standing, was now filling up with water, and we were all skidding around with the exception of Arthur, who was standing in the centre directing operations as rehearsed.

He ordered one of the heftier firemen to carry me off, and as this fireman bent down to pick me up in a fireman's grip, he lost his footing on the wet floor, went down and took me with him. This was all greatly enjoyed by the audience, and by this time I had got the 'giggles'. I couldn't keep my face straight – which was hardly in character – and could barely hear myself speak above the water which was being sprayed everywhere. It was also becoming more and more difficult to stand in the water that was by now all over the floor. The only way I could cover the laughter that was threatening to take hold of me was to pretend I was hysterical, so I shouted in a manic fashion at Arthur for his men to switch off the hose. Arthur sensed the situation and immediately yelled, 'Switch off', which was really an order to the real firemen on the other side of the studio. Then he took up the line in the rehearsed script which stated that I was suffering from 'fire-panic', and ordered the large fireman to pick me up again and rescue me. This gave me an opportunity to scream that I was all right, though I have never felt more like a drowned rat in my life. The big fireman put me down. With supreme effort I controlled my laughter, managed to act furious, and we continued with the rehearsed dialogue.

Another unrehearsed situation that occurred in one of the sketches in *The Arthur Haynes Show*, which stands out in my mind – probably because I will never forget the pain I felt as I tried to control my laughter, was set in a smart restaurant. I was dining on my own, and to my amazement a tramp comes in and sits at my table and starts chatting to me. I call the waiter to ask him to get the tramp to leave, only to be informed by the waiter in a whispered aside that this character is an eccentric millionaire in the same line of business as myself. I allow him to stay thinking it might be to my advantage. The tramp then produces his sandwiches, and suggests that we might share our 'dinners'. The sketch proceeds in this way but what had been overlooked was the fact that in rehearsal we did not have the real food and the eating had been mimed. Now on transmission Arthur had his thick sandwiches, and I had my plate of meat and salad. Those who remember *The Arthur Haynes Show* will not need to be told that one of the ploys of 'the tramp', Arthur Haynes, was always to try and get a good free meal.

As the sketch progressed, Arthur managed to get all the food off my plate on to his. The problem that had been overlooked was that before the sketch finished he was supposed to demolish nearly all the food, and drink most of the wine. It was one thing to speak with a full mouth, which in this situation was amusing in an embarrassing way, but when your mouth is full of food and you talk, it is impossible to swallow! In order to try and get most of the food off the plate and keep the sketch moving, Arthur kept shovelling more food into his mouth, but very little of it was being swallowed. In fact, some of it was coming back out of his mouth on to the plate in his efforts to carry on the dialogue. Arthur's cheeks bulged with uneaten food and the audience began to realise what was happening. Imagine the strain that I was feeling, sitting beside Arthur, and watching his discomfort at close hand, while at the same time trying to keep a straight face and sustain the pompous character I was playing. To make matters worse, the sketch was obviously over-running due to the increased laughter of the studio audience, and the fact that Arthur and I were both *ad-libbing* in order to hide the fact that the food wasn't being eaten. In the end he tried to swill down some of the unchewed food with the wine. This became even funnier, and the muscles of my stomach were knotted in pain with the effort to try and control my own laughter. We were by now receiving frantic messages from the studio manager to speed up in order that the programme could finish on time. We somehow managed to get our faces straight, Arthur swallowed most of the food and hiccuping we reached the end of the sketch, which had a marvellous pay-off. As Arthur spoke the line and the audience laughed, the producer cut to the ATV logo. There were no credits, no music, but we were 'out' on time.

In recent years, the programme *That's Life* has had more than its fair share of unexpected happenings, occasioned by Esther Rantzen's ability to be spontaneous on the air and also encourage others to be so. There was an hilarious occasion in one programme, in which Esther looked into a product which had come on the market called 'Sentoff'. The manufacturers claimed that once the dogs scented these particular pellets they immediately cleared off. A viewer had written to the programme complaining that far from sending off her dog, he had actually liked the tablets so much he had eaten them all. In order to test the product, Esther invited a number of viewers to come to the studio with their pet dogs. There must have been about twelve dogs, all of different breeds and different shapes and sizes in the studio. The production team had not realised what they had let themselves in for! The dogs completely ignored the tablets and began to wander aimlessly around the studio. One large Airedale took a passionate interest in a little Yorkshire Terrier and pursued it relentlessly around the studio in and out of the legs of the bemused dog owners. Most of the dogs were confused by the atmosphere, the lights and the audience's laughter, and two started snapping at each other. Esther tried to keep a straight face; her team got the giggles at the dogs' antics, and the climax was reached when one dog, seeing the only potted plant in the studio – right beside Esther's chair – and overcome with nerves, he cocked his leg and relieved himself in full view of the camera. The scent now arising from the potted plant got through to the other dogs who seemed to think that must be the reason for the presence of the potted plant, and followed the first leg cocker. The whole thing was getting out of control and Esther had to call for assistance in removing the dogs from the studio so she could get on with the rest of the show.

When they first started out, Morecambe and Wise were far from being the popular comedians that they eventually became. At first they couldn't even get an engagement, it was felt that they sounded too much like Jewel and Warriss. They did eventually land a broadcast, in a programme called *Fanfare*. This led to them being asked to appear in a television show. It was 1954 and the programme was called *Running Wild*. The reviews were horrific: Do those journalists now have egg on their faces, who wrote the following?

'How do two commonplace performers such as these get elevated to the position of having a series built round them?'

'How dare they put such mediocre talent on television.'

'Definition of the week. TV set – the box in which they buried Morecambe and Wise.'

One sketch Morecambe and Wise did concerned a taxi. Ernie was sitting in a taxi, which could not actually be driven off the set, but had to be hauled off by stage hands pulling a rope. When he was to move off, Ernie accidentally put the taxi into gear, with the result that it would not budge. This was a live show, and Eric was just standing there unable to continue the sketch – he started to *ad-lib*. Nothing happened, so he climbed in beside Ernie, still *ad-libbing*. Ernie *ad-libbed* back. Eric hissed to him what was wrong. Ernie did not understand. Eventually a hand appeared from nowhere – much to the viewers' amazement – altered the gear lever to neutral and the taxi was pulled off, with the producer no doubt pulling out his hair because of the time lost that would have to be picked up somewhere as the show progressed.

When Morecambe and Wise were booked to go on the *Ed Sullivan Show* in America with its audience of fifty-three million, they were naturally very excited. The reality was somewhat dampening. Ed Sullivan introduced them as Morrow, Camby and Wise, and said that they were a European Act. Eric and Ernie pointed out tactfully that they were British. The next time they appeared on Ed Sullivan's show, he had *Rule Britannia* played!

As always on television, scenery can be a problem. Among the many distinguished actors who have appeared on the *Morecambe and Wise Show* was Robert Hardy, who found a door coming away in his hand during a sketch, and Terry Wogan who found that one of the wall lights came off as he made his entrance! These are the kind of hiccups that Eric thrived on. Such happenings were meat and drink to a comedian like him. His brilliance as an *ad-libber* and his unique flair for taking the simplest situation and turning it to his advantage must be unrivalled. Sometimes it would 'corpse' the guest who was not used to such spontaneous performing. As when Hannah Gordon, wearing a dress with full sleeves was supposed to look at her watch but when she looked at her wrist she found that she had forgotten it. Eric picked it up immediately, and in his engagingly cheeky way tried to embarrass her.

'You haven't got your watch on, have you?' He turned to the audience and cried: 'She hasn't got her watch on, ladies and gentlemen. What an actress.' The audience laughed as poor Hannah struggled gamely to return to the script.

Cilla Black had a show in which she would move out of the studio into the streets with a camera unit. They would eventually land up at a house, knock on the door and get the inhabitants to come out, invite her in and be inter-viewed. In one programme the crew stopped outside a house. Cilla made her introduction to camera and then knocked on the door. The crew turned on more lights and Cilla asked the family to come out. Nothing happened, so Cilla *ad-libbed* while the stage manager knocked on the door again. The door opened a tiny bit and Cilla called out: 'Come on, luv, open up, it's Cilla Black here. Won't you ask us in for a word or two?' The door was opened, and the crew followed Cilla inside to find a number of embarrassed men sitting primly on a row of chairs. Cilla went on asking her questions, and received very terse replies. Later, after the programme was over, the team learnt that they had actually visited the local brothel!

On another occasion, when the lights went on outside a home, a couple came out on to the balcony of the house in utter disbelief. Cilla introduced herself, and then she real-

ised that the man was in his shirt only, and the woman had only a sheet wrapped round her. Later, they found out that the man was not the lady's husband – and they had been found *in flagrante delicto*.

Eddie Large, the lovable comedian of the 'Little and Large' comedy double act told me that one of their most embarrassing experiences was when they appeared on that long-running programme, *The Good Old Days*. They had been wanting to appear on this programme for some time, but the producer of the show, the very experienced Barney Colehan, thought that they were a little too modern for this particular programme. Eventually their agent managed to get them a booking, and they decided to do an old number of Ella Shields' called *He's Not All There*. This number suited them well, since Sid Little was able to come on stage looking gormless, and sing about the different things he had done with Eddie Large, ending each chorus with, 'He's not all there.'

They rehearsed the number meticulously, since they wished to make an impression in the programme and show Barney Colehan that he was wrong in thinking them too modern. Sid is a rather slow study, so for safety he had written the words of the lyric on the inside of his straw hat. The programme is recorded at the City of Varieties in Leeds, and when the time came for them to do their spot, Leonard Sachs, in his role as the Victorian Master of Ceremonies, gave his customary overblown and pompous introduction and the orchestra followed with their entrance music. As the curtains parted Eddie Large stepped forward, catching his foot somehow in a loop of rope. He could not disentangle himself and get on stage. The music went on playing and Eddie struggled behind the curtain to get the rope off his legs. He eventually freed himself and walked on to the stage, but it was not the best way to begin a number. Sid Little followed him on stage and the problem with the rope added to the nervousness he was already feeling, with the result that as soon as they began the number Sid forgot his lines. Remembering the precautions he had taken, he took off his hat to read them. Unfortunately, what he had overlooked was that he was wearing thick pebble-rimmed glasses to help create the gormless character he was playing and Sid is unable to read without his normal spectacles. He squinted inside the hat, but it was useless. Being an old pro, it was instinctive for him to keep going. He muttered some jumbled words in time to the music, to which Eddie Large tried to respond. Eddie told me how he thought that any minute Barney Colehan would stop the show and ask them to begin again as it was a recording. This didn't happen, so they assumed that what they were doing was coming across on the television, and being very experienced comedians the audience were certainly enjoying their confusion and *ad-libbing*. They actually went on for about ten minutes like this, though the number was only supposed to run four minutes. They didn't really feel the egg on their face until later when they watched the transmission to discover their 'spot' had been cut to a minute and a half!

Sid Little and Eddie Large have a very successful television series, and one time they were doing some filming in the streets of Hove on the Sussex coast. It was what we call a 'quickie', a short sketch of a minute or two with a strong pay-off. In this quickie sketch Eddie drew up in a car outside an optician's, leapt out with a mask over his face, threw a brick through the shop window, grabbed something from inside and got back into the car and drove off. At this moment Sid as a policeman walks into view, looks at the car driving away, looks at the shop window and then up at the sign which is written very large, OPTICIAN. He makes some reference to the fact that this is what he has been looking for and walks inside the shop, presumably to collect his new spectacles. The moment had come to film this scene. As usually happens when filming on location in the street, quite a crowd had gathered to watch the rehearsal. Once they came to what is known as 'the take', two members of the production team were delegated to stop passers-by walking across the area where they were filming. This was duly done, Eddie took his imitation rubber brick and got into the car ready to drive up to the optician's. The shot of the glass actually smashing would be done on a separate close-up and cut-in later. Eddie leapt out of the car and hurled his rubber brick. Unfortunately, at that precise moment a little old lady, who was probably short-sighted as well and had not seen what was taking place, managed to slip past the man who was holding back the passers-by and walked into the camera's view. At the sight of Eddie dressed as he was, and throwing the brick at the window, she screamed. It was quite a while before they could calm her down and reassure her that it was just a scene that was being acted out for television.

Rolf Harris, one of the most delightful people in show business, landed his first evening variety show in this country. The year was 1967 and the programme was still going out 'live'. He experienced what must be one of the most embarrassing things that can happen to an entertainer. It is bad enough when this situation occurs in the theatre, but when it is on television before millions and in close-up, it is devastating. Rolf had just finished one of his own numbers, and as the applause died down he began to introduce the next artist, who was the singer Shani Wallis. He gave her a big build-up, listing some of her singing and acting credits, and finished the introduction by reminding the audience and viewers of her recent success in the musical film, *Oliver*. As he was saying this, the music began, and he turned with his hand outstretched in the direction from where she was going to make her entrance, but could not remember her name. For some strange reason the name that came to mind was that of another singer popular at the time, Vicki Carr. He knew this was wrong, and through the orchestral introduction he mumbled something, and Shani swept on to begin her number. Fortunately, she never realised that her name had not been mentioned before she began and Rolf was able to come back immediately she had finished and let the viewers know in loud clear tones who had been entertaining them. As he said, 'It's bad enough making a mistake like that on the stage, but on television, in close-up, you feel the roots of your hair standing up, the blood draining from your face, the sweat on your hands, and your stomach turning to jelly. To say there is "egg on your face" is putting it mildly!'

Rolf has had a number of children's programmes, both in this country and in his native Australia. He has a great way with children, but he always remembers an incident from one of the earlier programmes he did. It was in 1958, and the programme was called *B for Birthday*, and transmitted weekly at 5 p.m. by ATV from their Aston Studios in Birmingham. In the programme he encouraged children in the studio to play party games. One particular game was word association. On reflection he wonders whether some of the children had difficulty understanding his Australian accent. He hadn't been in the country long, and he was still finding that the Birmingham accent could sometimes be a little puzzling. On this occasion he had a group of really rough young characters, most of whom had a very thick accent. He was playing the word association game, and finding it rather heavy going. He said, 'Now when I mention roast beef, what is the first word that you think of?' There was silence. He was expecting them to say: 'Yorkshire Pudding'. Surely, he thought, every English child knows about roast beef and Yorkshire Pudding? He tried again. 'What is the first thing you think of when I say roast pork?' He expected them to say, 'Apple sauce'. There was silence. Again he thought, surely, every English child had heard of roast pork and apple sauce. He was becoming desperate. He said, 'What word do you associate with cops?' Hands immediately went up, and back came the reply in thick Birmingham accents, 'Saucers'.

Technical hitches can create all kinds of embarrassing moments for artists, and if you haven't the experience or ability to *ad-lib* your way out of the situation, you are often left with 'egg on the face'. If your early experience has been on live television and radio, then one's instinct is always to keep going, and try and cover the mistake. I had one of these experiences when I was recording an edition of *Super*

Troupers for Tyne Tees Television, which was transmitted in February 1985. The programme was recorded at the beautiful little Tyne Theatre in Newcastle, and I was performing a monologue. I had almost reached the end, when for no apparent reason the stand microphone at which I was working suddenly descended. I had no option but to stop, and my reaction was to watch it go down in amazement, which seemed to amuse the audience. I assumed by this time that the producer of the show was going to stop the recording. Almost immediately the microphone rose from the boards again, which the audience thoroughly enjoyed since any technical hitch seems to entertain them. I made a rather bawdy *ad-lib* about the microphone which fitted in with the material I had been performing. I was not concerned because I thought that by this time the recording had been stopped. This interruption had affected my 'flow', and I got my words thoroughly confused. I thought that if they were recording, the tape would be edited to make sense, so I picked up where I had left off. My words came out even more jumbled, which amused the audience, and I took the opportunity to capitalise on the situation and at the same time *ad-lib* my way out of it. I eventually delivered the final verse with the correct words, and imagined that it would be edited in at the moment that the microphone unexpectedly descended to the floor. Imagine my embarrassment when I watched the transmission of the show to discover that most of the mistakes and *ad-libbing* had been kept in. I thought the producer might have cut it out and sent it to the programme: *It'll be Alright on the Night*.

On one occasion in *Crackerjack* the children's television series, one of the actors began to feel very ill – he had had a less-than-fresh chicken for lunch. He was appearing in a sketch and the man he was acting with realised that something was amiss, so *ad-libbed* a cue, enabling the first man to leave the scene. He just managed to get out of camera shot but not clear of the set, when the inevitable happened, much to the delight of the audience!

On another occasion in *Crackerjack*, Michael Aspel, who

used to introduce the programme, had a bad experience
with a cake. It seemed straightforward enough; Frankie
Howerd was joking with Michael, who then had to cut this
giant cake. Then it was decided that the cake should be a
twelve-foot swimming pool filled with crazy foam. Frankie
would hand Michael the knife, the cake would be cut and
Michael would be pushed in! It was not, of course, possible
for the stunt to be rehearsed. At the end of the show the
cast and some children mounted the dais. Frankie said his
lines and asked Michael if he would like a slice.

'I'm looking forward to this,' replied Michael.

'Right, then you can have the lot,' replied Frankie, giving
Michael a shove. The children also pushed, with the result
that Michael was given a bigger push than necessary. He
went flying through the air, and plunged through the foam
like a knife through butter and hit the hard floor below! He
was stunned! Eventually he got his breath back and surfaced. Afterwards the producer congratulated him on his
sense of timing, 'You stayed under so long – it was very
funny.'

Unfortunately, in being 'funny' Michael had broken a
wrist and cracked his head open. Returning to Broadcasting
House, he met the director of *Crackerjack* who, while being
sympathetic, moaned about the accident report, and all the
paperwork it involved.

One of this country's most successful and popular comedians is Max Boyce. Part of his success has undoubtedly
been built on a Welshman's passion for rugby football. He
can inject such feeling and emotion into quite a simple story
about this great game, he can raise a laugh where a lesser
comic with the same material might fail to register at all.
His love of this game, however, once landed him in a situation which left him standing with the proverbial egg all over
his animated Welsh features.

Some time in the early 1970s, the BBC had commis-
sioned him to write a topical song about the Wales–France
Rugby International. He was appearing on a programme on
Welsh Television, which started immediately after the game

in Paris ended. The idea was for him to sing the song at the top of the programme thus making it almost a news item. In his own words . . . 'To cover all eventualities, I had written two songs – one a song of celebration, should Wales win, and another a lament, if Wales had lost. We rehearsed the two songs all day and taught the studio audience both choruses, until they were word perfect. You can imagine my feeling of despair, when Wales and France drew 13 all!' There was no time to rehearse a third version. He just muddled through as best he could, and being the great professional that he is no one was aware of the embarrassment he felt.

10 · Documentaries

I am sure that the average viewer, on watching a documentary, thinks what an interesting and fascinating time the film crew must have had making the film. Travelling to exciting places they could never hope to visit and seeing unusual and sometimes exotic events. They seldom think of the conditions under which that crew might be living, the dangers to which they might be exposed on occasions, not to mention the long and lonely periods away from home and family.

That marvellous programme, *Survival*, originates from Anglia Television. When it first started in the early 1960s, it was not usual, as it is today, to catch animals by shooting them with tranquilliser darts first. A film crew had a frightening experience when filming a rhino hunt. Rhinos are extremely dangerous beasts and charge with great speed and power. The rhino hunters explained to the film crew that it was 'every man for himself' – if they fell off the truck they would be left to fend as best they could. The first rhino was a fairly docile creature, and catching her and her calf was comparatively easy. It just entailed chasing them for two miles, at great speed, mowing down trees that got in the way, until the two animals were lassoed.

The next rhino was a different matter. The trucks used were open ones, with tree trunks lashed back and front to reduce the impact of a rhino charge. The driver tried to drive alongside the rhino, who was going at some speed, and the catchers attempted to loop a stout rope over the rhino's head. There was a lot of shouting of instructions, and the truck bounced around and shook like mad, but the animal managed to escape. A larger rhino was sighted, and the truck went off in pursuit, bouncing and bucking along the rocks and trees. The film crew were, to put it mildly, rather frightened. They drew alongside this enormous rhino who, without slackening speed, gave the truck two terrific biffs with her sharp horn. Then the catchers discovered that the lasso wouldn't fit over the rhino's head, but after the rope was adjusted, they finally succeeded. The rhino, not liking this at all, tried to shake herself free, tossing her head up and down. The catchers quickly wrapped the rope round a solid-looking tree. The driver then drove the truck round her to try to stop her straining and then back away towards the tree so that she could be more securely roped.

Suddenly the rhino charged sideways, the rope whipped against the windscreen, and the cameraman was confronted nose to nose with a very angry large animal. The rhino swerved away from the truck but her horn hit the body of the cab. The animal detached herself, and ran round to the front of the truck butting it for all she was worth.

One of the rhino catchers coolly got out of the truck and put a rope over her hindquarters. When these were firmly held she stopped struggling and calmed down. All the time, the cameramen John Buxton and Chiels Margash were calmly filming. Such is the strange world of television that when the crew returned to England, those sitting comfortably in their offices complained of the poor quality of the filming – too much 'camera shake' I suppose!

The cameramen who film wild-life films are always in danger – they face, not only charging rhinos, but charging elephants as well. Even fairly docile animals become interested in cameras.

Dieter Plage, a distinguished film maker, recalls one such incident in the village of Vitshumbi in the National Park in Zaire. In the village there are some fairly tame elephants who wander around quite freely. The bull elephant was particularly friendly, letting the children, so it was said, swing on its tusks. When Dieter Plage and his crew arrived, the elephant had temporarily left the village and gone to live nearby on the edge of the lake. They began filming it there which seemed to annoy the elephant. As the elephant charged, Dieter decided it was time to move – but he was wearing a heavy battery needed to power his camera. As he began to run, the lead from the battery pulled the camera and tripod over. This probably saved him, as the elephant stopped to examine the camera and to trample on it with evident satisfaction. Dieter released himself from the battery and escaped, happy not to be as flat as the equipment on which the elephant was wiping its feet.

Alan Root is a cameraman of great distinction who lives in Kenya and often uses a light aircraft to get him from his home in Naivasha to remote parts of Africa. He has had scores of dangerous moments, once colliding in mid-air with a pack of vultures. On another occasion Alan Root, with his wife Joan, was filming hippo in Mzima Springs. One of the bulls got somewhat agitated and began moving away, stirring up a lot of mud. The humans waited patiently underwater for the mud to clear, but the bull spotted the bubbles they were making. He charged towards them and hit Joan, throwing her up and out of the water, his teeth piercing her rubber face mask, smashing the glass visor. He then bit Alan on the behind, and then went for Alan's right leg, biting his calf and wounding him badly. Though he had lost his mouthpiece Alan stayed underwater for as long as he could and luckily when he surfaced the hippo had got bored and left.

Animals are bad enough but humans can cause just as much embarrassment to the 'investigative journalist'. Michael Barratt, a very experienced and professional interviewer, remembers learning the hard way. It always seems so easy to get people arguing on a discussion programme but what if they don't.

Once, as a very new reporter on *Panorama*, he was detailed to chair a live debate on an increase in M.P.s' pay. It was, at the time, a highly controversial subject, and Tom Driberg and Charles Curran, two M.P.s who were supposed to have strong and opposing opinions on the subject were

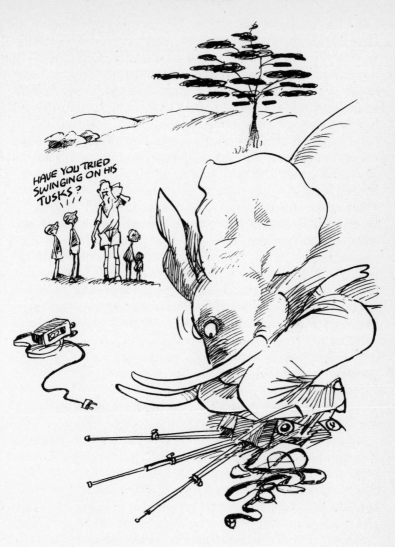

asked to appear. Barratt thought that he would have to dampen down the discussion and not contribute too much himself. He asked his first question and to his dismay the two M.P.s agreed with him, and each other. There was not much else that could be said, and as he was inexperienced at the time, he did not have the skill to turn this agreement into a balanced argument. So, rather sheepishly, Barratt had to sign off after only a minute or two of over polite chat.

Soon afterwards he had another disastrous brush with a politician – this time with the then Minister of Transport, Ernest Marples, who came to the studio having had to leave a very good dinner party. One of his aides took Barratt on one side and explained that the Minister was very tired and should be treated gently. Marples was not taken to the hospitality room, but when he arrived in the studio the Minister asked for a drink. The floor manager said there was nothing but water, which didn't seem to please Mr Marples. Barratt decided to start the questioning gently. 'Minister, this report calls for planning on a national basis. I'm surprised that you endorse its findings, because you are in principle opposed to this kind of planning.'

'When have I said that?' the Minister snapped.

Barratt hesitated.

'Come on, Mr Barratt, I want chapter and verse. Quote me the time and place that I have opposed planning.'

Barratt couldn't and was asked to withdraw the question. But he was still in deep water for the Minister truculently replied to the next question:

'You don't appear to understand the nature of our problem. Do you know the number of cars *per* mile of highway in Great Britain compared to the figure in the United States?'

Barratt hoped it was a rhetorical question but the Minister pressed on, 'Do you?'

And so the interview went on with Barratt getting the worst of the encounter. As he admits, he was rightly reprimanded later for not being sufficiently prepared and for permitting himself to be trounced by a politician who ought to have been the one with egg on his face.

Another embarrassing Barratt interview concerned an arms dealer. Michael calls him Captain X and says when he rang X he found him very frank, and to questions like: 'To whom do you sell arms?', replied, 'To anyone who wants to buy them, of course. We're doing particularly good trade in the Congo at the moment.'

'Which side?'

'To both of course. That's no concern of mine. I'm in the business to make money like anyone else.'

'And the Yemen?'

'Yes, that's a particularly good area just now. Both the Royalists and the Republicans. Very good customers they are.'

After further conversation Captain X agreed that he would come to Broadcasting House to be interviewed. Once again Michael asked his questions:

'Captain X, I understand you sell quantities of arms abroad. Can you tell me where they go?'

The Captain replied: 'Yes, the Belgians are perhaps our best customers. We've sent some big orders to France, too.'

'Anywhere else?' persisted Barratt. 'The Congo, for example, or the Yemen?'

'Good gracious no. I wouldn't do that. It would be most improper,' replied the arms dealer blandly and there was nothing further Michael could say.

David Attenborough, everyone's favourite 'animal man', discovered that the departments of the BBC could give as much trouble as the wild life. He was filming in South America, and in order to reach a remote part of the country he had to buy horses to transport his film crew and equipment. After filming, he and his crew, still on horseback, were taken by the tribal chief to a road, two-days' ride away, where they could get cars to take them back to civilisation. On leaving the Chief and his elders, who had guided them to this road, Attenborough was touched to receive gifts from them. Having nothing else to give in return David presented the tribesmen with the horses for which they no longer had a use.

He put the price of the horses on his expense sheet back home – it was quite a small amount. But the accountants were not pleased, and quoted a Corporation rule: 'Purchased goods or materials must remain the property of the Corporation, and shall be delivered by the claimant to the Corporation.' David was told that he must produce the animals or give some explanation, satisfactory to the accountants, why he could not do so. In splendid style, David wrote a succinct memo, which satisfied the accountants. It read simply: 'We ate them.'

Desmond Wilcox once had what he thought was going to be a very pleasant assignment for *ABC at Large*. The idea was to find out how much a night out cost in the company with a pretty girl. It all took place in Manchester and the girl, the chocolates, the flowers and the nightclub were all laid on by the television company. The programme would show Wilcox and the girl arriving at the club; Wilcox would explain to the viewers what was to happen; then throughout the programme he would, on cue, say how much he was spending and on what. It all seemed very simple. There was the usual chaos at the nightclub with technicians sorting out cameras, the electricity, the sound and all the other problems that go with an outside broadcast like this, but everything seemed to be in order as the time of the transmission approached. The nightclub owner offered Wilcox a substantial sum of money to mention the name and address of the club on the air, but Wilcox naturally refused. The stage manager, however, had disappeared and didn't appear until just before transmission – having accepted too much hospitality and being much the worse for drink. Wilcox, justifiably enraged, yelled at him, 'Get your effing finger out!' – then noticed, to his extreme chagrin that the red light on the camera was on and his words were being broadcast. He hurriedly went into his prepared introduction. There were lots of telephone calls afterwards, but most people thought that it was a new and lively title for the programme, and one caller asked for the telephone number of the blonde accompanying Wilcox!

Nationwide once heard about a duck that followed a farmer's wife around, even going shopping with her. This talented duck also used to make a barking sound at every dog and cat it met. This was a heaven-sent opportunity to obtain an amusing film item. The order was given to load up the vans, and the film crew drove rapidly to the farm, and right up to the farmhouse door. The director explained to the astonished lady why they had come and who they were. She looked past him at the cameramen unloading their cameras, the electricians and everyone busy about their jobs. She appeared so upset that the director asked her what was the matter. She cried, 'It's Dabber. Dabber my duck.' Asked what was the matter with him, she went on, 'You've just run over him!'

Esther Rantzen was arrested once while making a film for *That's Life*. She gets out on to the streets regularly for the programme to ask people's opinions on various topics or products. On this occasion she was inviting people's reactions to bat stew and went to the street market in North End Road, which is the spot she usually uses. The team stand on a corner, and only people who want to join in are filmed. The bat stew was decanted into little bowls, and Esther started her interviews, just as she had done many times before. Two policemen walked up and told her to move back. Esther asked why, and was told she was blocking the whole pavement. 'I've been doing this for twelve years,' she protested. One of the policemen said that she wasn't going to do it today. She and the team and the interviewee retreated down a nearby side street. The policemen followed: 'I told you to move,' said the Law. 'But I have,' said Esther. The policemen warned her and left. Esther and the film crew moved across to another corner and went on with the programme. This corner was bigger, and there was plenty of room for anyone to pass. In fact, mothers with babies in prams, old ladies with baskets and trolleys, a whole host of people were passing by. A black Maria arrived, Esther was arrested. She was driven to Fulham Police Station and charged with obstruction. She was fined £15.

P.S.

No book of broadcasting clangers and hiccups would be complete without a mention of that most lovable of newscasters, Reginald Bosanquet, who usually looked as if he were just about to drop a clanger – but seldom did. The night before he resigned he read his last news bulletin with Anna Ford. As she was reading the last item of news, Reggie wrote her a touching little poem. It seems a fitting post-script to this book.

> If I suffer from eccentricity,
> Do I have eggentricity
> on my face?
> I may not be here tomorrow
> Can I borrow
> All of your best wishes?